PERFECT
ENGLISH
GRAMMAR

For general information on our other products and services or to obtain technical support, please contact our Customer Care Department within the U.S. at (866) 744-2665, or outside the U.S. at (510) 253-0500.

Zephyros Press publishes its books in a variety of electronic and print formats. Some content that appears in print may not be available in electronic books, and vice versa.

ISBN: Print 978-1-62315-714-2 | eBook 978-1-62315-715-9

PERFECT ENGLISH GRAMMAR

THE INDISPENSABLE GUIDE TO EXCELLENT WRITING AND SPEAKING

Grant Barrett

ZEPHYROS PRESS

CONTENTS

1.0
GENERAL PRINCIPLES 16

2.0
COMPOSITION 19

3.0
PARTS OF SPEECH
DEFINED 36

4.0

SPELLING AND FORMATTING ... 39

5.0

SENTENCE STRUCTURE 73

6.0

VERBS 84

7.0

DETERMINERS 109

8.0

NOUNS

9.0

ABBREVIATIONS

10.0

PRONOUNS

11.0

ADJECTIVES 157

12.0

ADVERBS 164

13.0

PREPOSITIONS 168

14.0

CONJUNCTIONS 172

15.0

INTERJECTIONS 176

16.0

17.0

INTRODUCTION

I grew up in rural Missouri. My father was a cop. My mother was an Avon lady. They raised five kids to be clean, be quiet, and be good (with mixed results for "quiet" and "good"). Education was mostly left to the schools. There were no tutors, no college prep, no books on how to help children succeed at life. It worked out for me somehow: I became a constant reader, and with the help of libraries, I added to my learning.

But nobody emphasized for me that writing and speaking well were important until I was in my twenties. In grade school and high school—where I felt I excelled at composition and literature analysis—everything seemed fine. It was about overall literacy, the broad strokes of language. I listened, I did the work, and I passed the tests.

But in college, that wasn't enough. Others noticed I used too many commas. Professors left embarrassing remarks about my writing on my essays. The student newspaper editors cut my wordiness to tight journalistic paragraphs that I couldn't seem to come up with on my own.

Clearly, there was a higher level of attention I could pay to my writing and speaking. So, I set out to fix my language.

There was so much I didn't know.

It turned out to be so interesting I dived in deep and eventually became a lexicographer—someone who compiles and edits dictionaries—especially dictionaries for people learning English through classwork rather than by being born into it.

Later, I became the co-host of a public radio show about words and language now heard by more than 500,000 people a week around the world. Now, I give speeches, I talk to the press about language (especially about new words and slang), and, as you can see, I write books about it. I want others to see what I see: with a little bit of help, anyone can improve their communication.

Since you're reading this, there's a good chance you or someone you know needs help with their language. To help as many people as possible, I've written this book to be useful for a wide range of readers, writers, and learners: junior high, high school, and college students; graduate students who speak English as a second (or even third) language; or business professionals and community leaders who need a refresher on grammar points they last thought about decades ago.

This book does not cover all of English grammar. Instead, it contains frequently asked questions I've encountered from writers, speechmakers, and language learners of all ages and kinds. It also includes facts that were eye-openers for me when I first started on my journey of communicating better. I hope this book will be your trusted companion as you express all that you have to say.

HOW TO USE
THIS BOOK

▬

First, browse the book to familiarize yourself with its contents. Then, when questions come up, use the table of contents and the index to find answers. Each entry has an index number. Related subjects appear near each other or are mentioned in a cross-reference like this: see section 8.0, Nouns.

I know many readers like to dip and skim for pleasure, so I've written this book so you can open to any page, read for a few minutes, and go away with a little nugget of information. Of course, you can read the whole thing straight through, too, if that's your style. I don't judge.

To make everything easier to understand, I've included example sentences, lists and charts, and a glossary explaining some of the specialized language of grammar and linguistics.

WHAT DOES THIS BOOK MEAN BY "PERFECT GRAMMAR"?

lthough this book features the word *grammar* in the title, it also pays a lot of attention to things that aren't strictly grammar (at least in the academic linguistic sense of the word). You'll find information on writing well, spelling, style, usage, and more.

Grammar does not exist alone: it is just one of the complex ways we communicate with each other. So, this book will also motivate you to improve your communication by using correct basic grammar as a framework around finding your own voice, which, in short, is about figuring out who you are, what you want to say, who you want to say it to, and how best to do it.

"Perfect" is what we shoot for but never achieve. It's a short-hand for constantly working to improve your writing and speech while acknowledging that perfection is subjective. Try for perfect communication, but give yourself a break if you're not there yet.

I encourage you to think about the contents not as "grammar rules" but as "grammar guidelines." My goal is to help you make the best choice for your situation without having to fear somebody will hunt you down and make fun of you because you did it your way instead of their way.

In fact, if you try to follow all the rules or guidelines exactly, you will likely make a mess of your writing. There are few unassailable rules—you just have to become experienced enough to know when to challenge them.

I also encourage you to work on developing your *speaker's intuition*. This is a fancy way of saying "your natural understanding of what is acceptable in English." This is done by making it a daily habit to read and listen to many different writers and speakers who are a little more advanced than you are, and by consulting this book (and books like it) whenever you are in doubt.

If, after using this book for a while, you feel as though you've learned everything it has to teach you, go on to the books mentioned in the Further Reading section on page 227. They're works I know, by authors I trust, that offer practical advice anyone can use, even if you're not a professional grammarian.

Grant Barrett
SAN DIEGO, CALIFORNIA | 2016

1.0

GENERAL PRINCIPLES

PRINCIPLES

These guidelines should help you make the most of this book as you work toward becoming a better writer.

1. Consistency matters. When you make a style choice, stick with it throughout your project. When you choose a tense (see section 6.4), person (see section 6.1), or tone, think twice before switching to a new one.

2. English offers many options. There may be more than one acceptable choice. There isn't necessarily just one answer for every language dilemma.

3. Words can have more than one meaning and more than one use. Be wary.

4. English is illogical in places. Trying to make it logical is a mistake. Instead, bend to it.

5. There is a variety of linguistic terms for the same features of English. It is more important to understand the concepts than to know all the terms.

6. Write for your audience (see section 2.2.1) rather than for yourself. Write appropriately for the situation.

7. Write to be understood. Don't let anyone's rules get in the way of good communication.

8. Avoid doing things differently than everyone else. It can distract from your message. This especially applies to beginning or nonfluent writers, as they often reach beyond their abilities.

9. Avoid the urge to put writerly tricks to work unless they come naturally to you. Simple does it. Before literary writers could do clever things with their work, they had to understand the ordinary ways of language. Basic language rules underlie everything they write.

10. Use a thesaurus only to remind yourself of words you already know. Don't use a thesaurus to find new words for your writing. You are very likely to misuse new words, because a thesaurus does not always indicate which words are appropriate for which contexts.

11. Throughout this book, I recommend consulting a dictionary. Consider using two dictionaries from different publishers. Each dictionary has its own strengths. Be sure to use dictionaries from well-known publishers, as off-brand dictionaries tend to be out-of-date and less thorough. See my recommendations in the Further Reading section (page 227).

12. Use the style guide preferred by your organization, school, teacher, or industry and stick with it. Well-known style guides sometimes disagree on specifics. In this book, I give guidelines that will, generally, work for everyday writing for school and work.

13. Use the table of contents, the index, and the glossary. This is not only a browsable book, but also one that can be used for easy lookups.

2.0

COMPOSITION

COMPOSITION

Writing well is one of the most crucial tools of the modern person. It is a skill required by nearly every profession, and one that allows you to get your work done, help others, and leave behind a legacy of your thoughts and actions so you may be remembered long after you are gone.

2.1 A Few Words of Advice

Think of words as bricks and boards, sentences as walls and windows, paragraphs as houses, and essays, stories, and articles as neighborhoods. Your writing is a little world for your readers, which you furnish in a way that, you hope, delights them.

Writing is a learned process that doesn't come naturally to anyone. We all must be taught it. Don't fret if you think you're behind where you should be. You can learn it, just as many millions of people have before you. Hang in there.

Writing has different rules than speaking does. What naturally comes out of our mouths may seem fine to us, but if we write it down exactly as we speak it, other people—who can't see our memories, emotions, knowledge, and ideas—will get only vague, misshapen impressions of what we mean. We must write differently than we speak.

Writing is messy. I know many authors and writers, and none of them writes anything meaningful without planning, revising, and editing. There is a myth of the genius writer who can do it all perfectly in one try. Do not think you're failing if you can't do that. Also, everybody needs a good editor. Everybody!

It's easy to lose sight of what is important. You focus on word count rather than results. You lose track of your good idea because you're worried about margins or type size. You're concerned about the introduction but haven't given a thought to the conclusion. You're so worried about your deadline it distracts you from doing the work. Many writers go through this! You are not alone. To focus on what is important, look at the finished, published writing around you and think, "If they did it, so can I."

Format at the end. Things like bolding, italicizing, and setting margins can be distractions from what matters most. You'll end up having to redo a lot of the formatting, anyway.

Writing well isn't magic. Even large parts of the most superb award-winning books have been perfunctory or even mechanical. Sometimes simply following the steps will get you to the end. You don't always need inspiration. Sometimes you simply need to sit down, do it, and stop worrying.

2.2 Getting Started

For some people, the hardest part of writing is the blank page, that looming, scary place where nothing seems to be happening, and nothing in your head seems good enough to put down.

2.2.1 WRITE FOR THE CORRECT AUDIENCE

I once worked with a young person who couldn't write light, fun emails for clients because he was still stuck in the university essay mode. Everything came out in a formal tone. I've also seen new students who should know better send very casual emails to their professors, completely lacking in even the simplest of composition niceties, such as capital letters, punctuation, or even "please" and "thank you." Don't be the person who doesn't recognize when it is the right time for formal versus informal language! Match the tone and register of your audience.

2.2.2 OPENING SENTENCES CAN BE HARD, BUT THEY DON'T HAVE TO BE

If you're having trouble putting down your first words, try these ideas. They can also break up writers' block.

Build a structure first. Plan. Use a spreadsheet, outline, or graph paper. You'd be surprised how many writers of all kinds—speechwriters, newspaper reporters, novelists, screenplay writers, and so on—first sketch out their ideas in a structured form. Some use a slideshow program's outline view to build a structure on which they can hang all their ideas, and then easily rearrange them by moving slides around. Use your big ideas as headings. Then break those down into their component parts. Then explain those parts with sentences.

Just write. Write anything. Write what you ate for breakfast. Just get started putting something on that blank page. Break that psychological barrier. Know it's not going to be perfect yet and be fine with that. It is fine. I promise. You can cut or edit it later (see section 2.8). But for now, these are your first lines, you did them, and that's something.

Write a complete plot summary as your first line. For example:

- There are solid reasons you and your party members should completely support State Bill 301b and join our coalition in urging the governor to sign it.
- She was a wicked woman, but purely so, and by the time she ruled the enchanted forest, she'd forgotten what it was like to love.
- When I think about myself a few years down the road, I see myself working at Lexxtopia, Inc., managing a team of software developers, and making the best mobile software on the market.

Tell someone else about your writing. Some people feel that talking to anyone else will void their ideas of meaning, that in the telling, the magic is gone, and all that is left is dusty vagueness. But the important part is to ask the other person to tell your ideas back to you. You'll probably find yourself wanting to correct what they're saying, or add to their words. As the two of you discuss your project, take notes. Take lots of notes as quickly as you can. Those notes become your outline.

Start at the end. If your hero dies in the end, write that first. Then, write what happened right before the hero died. And then write what happened before that. Keep working backward until you reach the beginning of the story. This also works for speeches, essays, and even complicated emails: put down your final, summarizing thoughts, and then justify them.

Write the fun part first: the big love scene, the explanation of all the convincing survey data, the recital of the project that won you a promotion, the anecdote that perfectly illustrates the spirit of what you're doing.

Write simply. Write below your level of learning. Write for a five-year-old. Don't try to write the most educated first line ever. Write to be understood. Write what helps you understand what your goals are: Who is your audience? What do you want? What do they want? Who are the characters? What motivates them?

Tell it like gossip or a family memory. Begin as if you're at a family reunion, or on the front porch, or at the hair salon, or as if you're an old-timer who wants to pass something along to the youngsters:

- There's a story I've been meaning to tell you. It's about . . .
- When I think back to that time, I remember feeling . . .
- When I was a child, I had just one goal. It was . . .

Make a puzzle for yourself. Think of yourself as both a puzzle-maker and a puzzle-solver. You don't know which paragraph will be the first one until you've written them all down and can see what's what. Then, you can rearrange each of the bits until you find a pleasing order. Hunter S. Thompson was known for sending his stories to the editors of *Rolling Stone* in long streams of faxes. Once in the office, the faxes were cut into pages and paragraphs, and then rearranged on the floor: editing was like solving a jigsaw puzzle.

2.3 Paragraph Structure

In this section, we are concerned mainly with writing essays and similar formal or quasi-formal documents read by authority figures such as teachers or bosses. However, even in the most literary writing (as you can see in the examples near the end of this section), the formal rules can still work very well.

A **paragraph** is the foundation of writing structure. In many ways, it mimics the larger structure of a typical essay. Each paragraph contains one or more sentences, which generally cover one subject.

In formal writing, there are three parts to a paragraph:

1. topic
2. body
3. conclusion

This is a *general* structure. Different kinds of writing can condense or stretch this form from one sentence to a page of paragraphs.

Besides those three parts, paragraphs have two important characteristics:

1. They contain one main idea.
2. They have multiple sentences.

How do you know when to start a paragraph?

- when introducing an essay or a new idea
- when concluding an essay or finishing the discussion of an idea

- when an existing paragraph seems to contain too many ideas (in which case, move each main idea into its own paragraph)
- when trying to avoid a big unbroken block of words—or "wall of text"—which can be intimidating

Paragraphs can be any length, but good writers usually try to break down long paragraphs into several shorter paragraphs. No matter how long a paragraph is, it should have a reason to be there, and have a job to do (a job that isn't simply about making the writing longer, or trying to impress the reader). Broken-out shorter paragraphs are stylistic, but they can still contain discrete ideas. Just look carefully at your words and figure out where the natural separation points are.

2.3.1 PARAGRAPH TOPIC

The topic sentence for a paragraph is usually the first sentence. It should be broad, with just enough information to introduce the ideas that will be explained in more detail within the paragraph, or in other paragraphs. In more sophisticated writing, or in a longer essay, the topic sentence (or topic phrase) can appear anywhere in the paragraph, but it is always there.

2.3.2 BODY AND SUPPORTING SENTENCES

The **body** is where the majority of the paragraph's work is done. It explains more specifically what was hinted at in the topic sentence, and answers any questions that may have appeared in the reader's mind. The supporting sentences not only explain, but also justify the topic sentence: they give proof to its statements, legitimize it, analyze it, and break it down into smaller, explainable parts.

There are many kinds of good supporting sentences:

- descriptions
- data, such as statistics
- quotes or paraphrases of others' words
- examples
- definitions of important terminology
- contrasts and comparisons
- a timeline or step-by-step report of what happened

2.3.3 NUMBER OF SENTENCES IN A PARAGRAPH

In elementary and high school composition classes, you may have been told the body of a paragraph should have three, five, seven, or more supporting sentences. By all means, follow your teachers' instructions and give them what they want.

But just know that these specific numbers are not connected to what English grammar requires. The English language doesn't care how many sentences you use.

Your teachers tell you how many sentences to use per paragraph because they know if they say, "Write a five-paragraph essay," some students will write five three-sentence paragraphs (and short sentences, at that), and consider themselves done.

What they're trying to do is get you to write fully, in detail, and to find the natural flow of your writing so you stop only when the conclusion is honestly reached.

2.3.4 CONCLUSION

The concluding sentence summarizes what has been said, or presents the natural final thought that should occur in the reader's mind when all the paragraph's ideas or actions are put together. Many times, the conclusion restates the topic sentence. In a story or other kind of sequential narrative, the conclusion tends to include consequences and outcomes. In other cases, the conclusion is an observation, which more or less says, "Given what we've learned in this paragraph, X is true, Y is not, and we don't know about Z."

2.4 Example Paragraphs

Let's illustrate all three parts of a paragraph using a passage from *The Wind in the Willows* by Kenneth Grahame. The numbers indicate [1] topic, [2] body, and [3] conclusion.

> *[1] But Mole stood still a moment, held in thought. [2] As one wakened suddenly from a beautiful dream, who struggles to recall it, and can re-capture nothing but a dim sense of the beauty of it, the beauty! Till that, too, fades away in its turn, and the dreamer bitterly accepts the hard, cold waking and all its penalties; [3] so Mole, after struggling with his memory for a brief space, shook his head sadly and followed the Rat.*

Notice how Grahame has done things that show his skill level. He's started the paragraph with a conjunction (see section 14.0). He's used a semicolon (see section 16.6) to lead into the conclusion (where most modern writers would have made it a new sentence; *The Wind in the Willows* was first published in 1908). He's used repetition in the narrative to give it almost a spoken-word feel: "the beauty of it, the beauty!" These things indicate he is skilled, but using them is not what makes him skilled. What makes him skilled is his ability to make the reader *feel the story*.

Grahame's use of "But" at the start of the sentence is probably something you've been told not to do in your writing. Too right! Why? Because beginning writers tend to overuse conjunctions at the starts of sentences, as they seem to provide easy continuity when you're not really sure how else to make your sentences connect. Grahame, however, uses conjunctions at the beginning of sentences sparingly, so they have a forceful impact rather than just being a bland paste that holds the sentences together into a paragraph.

Ernest Hemingway is a good example of a writer who explains complex ideas with simple language, as in this paragraph from *The Sun Also Rises*.

> *[1] The fiesta was really started. It kept up day and night for seven days. [2] The dancing kept up, the drinking kept up, the noises went on. The things that happened could only have happened during the fiesta. Everything became quite unreal finally and it seemed as though nothing could have any consequences. It seems out of place to think of consequences during the fiesta. All during the fiesta you had the*

feeling, even when it was quiet, that you had to shout any remark to make it heard. It was the same feeling about any action. [3] It was a fiesta and it went on for seven days.

Hemingway's writing is so simple that where most other writers would have used many more commas, he uses only a few. Also, note how he also uses repetition: the conclusion is almost a word-for-word echo of the first two sentences, which make up the paragraph's introduction. He uses the word *fiesta* so many times it's almost a chant. It's powerful! And the paragraph follows normal high school essay-writing structure very well.

2.5 The Five-Paragraph Essay

At the core of a lot of school writing is the five-paragraph essay. It's a basic writing structure that can be used in much larger sizes, too, to construct long articles and even books. You'll notice it's a more elaborate form of the structure of the basic paragraph. Here, though, we're providing rich detail, supporting the ideas in the introduction, and firmly wrapping it all up in a conclusion.

This is what a typical outline might look like. Use this as a framework to build your essay to its conclusion.

PARAGRAPH 1: INTRODUCTION PARAGRAPH

- Provide a general opening statement. Sometimes this is provocative, controversial, or surprising.
- Elaborate on your opening statement. You might provide background information; explain how it affects other people, things, or situations; or indicate why you've chosen it as your essay's subject.

- Give a specific statement of purpose or your topic, which can be your thesis, hypothesis, or main opinion.
- Offer a brief overview of what you will say in your body paragraphs.

PARAGRAPH 2: BODY PARAGRAPH 1
- Use the paragraph structure explained in section 2.3.
- Focus on the single most important argument, reason, or fact that supports your specific statement of purpose.
- Be sure to use data, examples, and anecdotes to reinforce your thesis.

PARAGRAPH 3: BODY PARAGRAPH 2
- Focus on your second-most important argument, reason, or fact.

PARAGRAPH 4: BODY PARAGRAPH 3
- Focus on your third-most important argument, reason, or fact.

PARAGRAPH 5: CONCLUSION
- Rephrase your specific statement of purpose.
- Emphasize why it is important.
- Refer back to the basic points of each paragraph.
- Explain how the reader should be feeling about your arguments.
- Generally wrap it up with a firm, assertive statement.
- Avoid ending with something trite like *The End* or *That's all I have to say*.
- Instead of ending with a question like, "Don't you agree that X is the best thing ever?" or "Don't you think a good person would support Y?" try restating it as an assertion: "X is the best thing ever." "A good person would support Y."

2.6 Transitions and Coherence

Writers at all levels have a hard time making an argument that flows naturally from beginning to end—that's why it's taught in schools! Good transitions can help fix that by making it feel more like a story and less like a pile of facts and opinions.

- Avoid simply jumping to the next topic.
- Transitions can appear in topic sentences, concluding sentences, or both.

Develop a variety of transition techniques and use them without shame. Every good writer has a stock of useful phrases to ease them through their writing. In fact, as you're reading, note how other writers move smoothly between ideas and see if those strategies will work for you, too.

Inside of sentences, these words and phrases can help you build good transitions:

- although
- as a result
- at first
- eventually
- finally

- however
- next
- now
- then

Between sentences, these words and phrases can provide good transitions:

- A good example of that is
- As I wrote above

- Eventually
- Finally

- For instance
- Furthermore
- However
- In addition
- In conclusion
- In fact
- Indeed
- Just as with X, the facts show that Y is also
- More importantly
- On the other hand
- Overall
- Therefore
- This is also the opinion of Dr. Z, who believes
- To illustrate
- To put it briefly
- To summarize
- With this in mind

Good transitions are likely to suggest themselves during editing. See section 2.8, Editing.

2.7 Common Essay Mistakes to Avoid

Don't wait until the end to make your best point. **Always lead with your best arguments.** Sometimes, mistakenly, writers have the urge to put their most powerful arguments last, with the idea they are laying a foundation of small arguments that will lead to a big, undeniable argument that will win over the reader. This is sometimes a successful rhetorical technique, particularly in speeches where audience members might be more invested in staying to hear everything you're going to say. With the written word, however, there's too much chance that if you don't lead with your strongest arguments, a reader will just skip everything else you've written. Get them at the start.

Your supporting paragraphs should be several sentences long, but don't worry about their exact length. Explain things until your point is well made.

Support your opinions with official data, research, and experts' opinions, which are more persuasive than your opinions alone. Sentences that begin with *I think* or *I feel* need more than your thoughts and emotions to back them up.

Avoid repeating yourself in the body paragraphs. See section 17.20, Wordiness.

Think twice about trying to be funny, unless you've been asked specifically to write a humorous essay. Most attempts at humor fail.

2.8 Editing

This isn't about *how* to edit. It's about *why* to edit. In short, we edit because we're human and we make mistakes. Editing means we look at our text with sharp eyes to find errors and to fix them.

The longer version is we edit because we make mistakes, and we make mistakes because:

- We've been staring at the same text for so long our eyes glide over errors.
- The ideas are clear in our heads, so our brains fill in the gaps where pieces are missing. Other people will notice the gaps right away.
- We frequently do not give ourselves enough time to do the work, because we underestimate the size of the task or because we waste time.

To edit your own work:

- If you can finish with lots of time to spare, put the writing aside and then go back to it later. Even just a couple of hours can give you a new perspective on your own work. If you can go back to it days or even weeks later, so much the better. It will be like reading someone else's work, and you're likely to say, "What was I thinking?" more than a few times.
- If you don't have time to spare, a widely used trick is to temporarily change the typeface and the size of the text and margins. Make the margins bigger and the text larger. This way, your eyes are less likely to glide over familiar-looking blocks of text.
- Don't be kind to your own writing. The saying in the writing business is, "kill your darlings." That means that any spot where you think you've been particularly brilliant is a spot where you should spend time making sure it's really as brilliant as you think it is. Chances are, it can be trimmed, reworded, or even removed altogether.

If you are working on a book, master's thesis, dissertation, or other large, important document, arrange for an editor, or at least a reader, in advance. You need someone on the outside to give you a frank assessment of your work. I once worked for a company where the chief partner thought because he was the boss of everyone, nobody had the right to edit his text. He was mistaken. His editorial staff saved him from many an embarrassing mistake. Everybody needs an editor!

3.0

PARTS OF
SPEECH DEFINED

STRUCTURE

Parts of speech are categories of words sorted by their roles within the structure of the language.

Most of us learn about parts of speech when we first learn to write. But what often escapes us is that these boundaries between parts of speech are fluid. Verbs (see section 6.0) can behave like nouns. Nouns (see section 8.0) can behave like adjectives. Adjectives (see section 11.0) can behave like adverbs (see section 12.0). Many parts of speech can act as interjections (see section 15.0). Sometimes, a word in a particular part of speech transforms into a new word permanently (see section 4.4, Affixes), and becomes another part of speech.

The parts of speech are briefly defined here, and then explained in more detail in relevant sections throughout this book.

- **Adjectives** modify or describe nouns. See section 11.0.
- **Adverbs** modify or describe adjectives, verbs, or other adverbs. See section 12.0.
- **Articles** are determiners that introduce nouns. See section 8.5.
- **Conjunctions** connect clauses or sentences together. See section 14.0.
- **Determiners** are words that control the meaning of a noun or noun phrase. See section 7.0.
- **Interjections** are brief and abrupt insertions into speech, usually expressing emotion. See section 15.0.
- **Nouns** refer to people, places, or things. See section 8.0.

- **Prepositions** give context to nouns in relationship to other nouns or to pronouns. See section 13.0.
- **Pronouns** replace nouns or noun phrases. See section 10.0.
- **Verbs** (see section 6.0) show action or an ongoing condition, and are part of the predicate (see section 5.1).

4.0

SPELLING AND FORMATTING

STRUCTURE

Spelling is how we put characters and letters in their generally accepted order to represent words.

Unfortunately, English spelling is a mess!

A lot of our most basic words are spelled in a way that made more sense centuries ago when English sounded differently. These days, though, the match between orthography (a fancy way of saying *spelling*) and pronunciation (the sounds we make with our mouths when we say a word) is sometimes lost.

The problem becomes worse because, in English, the written language has never been a perfect representation of the spoken language, which has many dialects that are difficult to accommodate. Even when they sometimes match, the spoken language changes relatively quickly and the written word changes relatively slowly. That match disappears over centuries as the spoken and written forms go increasingly out of sync.

4.1 Improve Your Spelling

Want to improve your spelling? Rather than doing drills or flash cards, read really interesting stuff just a little bit above your skill level.

For example, if you like science, instead of reading about new scientific developments in a daily newspaper, read about them in *New Scientist*, which is a magazine written at a higher reading level than most newspapers.

Or, if you usually read books about time-traveling cats written for young adults, try reading books about time-traveling cats written for adults. You will likely encounter more complicated, harder-to-spell words.

After a certain amount of time of repeatedly seeing those same hard words, they will start to seem easy and normal.

If you want to learn to spell a lot of words very fast, try this trick: Write them all into the craziest story you can imagine. Then read the story aloud to yourself and friends—but when you get to the words you need to learn, spell them out instead of saying them:

- Then Kazoo the Time-Traveling Wonder Cat s-u-b-j-u-g-a-t-e-d the poor Puppy Planet.

You'll discover when you're done that each word will be attached in your mind to a particular part of your strange story; those kinds of memory clues, or *mnemonics*, work because humans are much better at remembering stories than lists of facts.

When you look up words in the glossary (see page 222) or in a dictionary, keep them in a list. Chances are, you're going to have to look them up again later: sometimes it takes as many as six look-ups for a newly learned spelling to stick. Your own personal World's Worst Words list will become like a mini-dictionary made just for you.

4.2 Common Spelling Errors

Spelling in English is a problem even for native speakers—even highly educated native speakers. Studies show that good spelling isn't necessarily a sign of intelligence; instead, spelling well has a lot more to do with repetition and practice, and can be learned even by people of ordinary intelligence.

One reason English's spelling can be hard to master is the tangled etymological history I mentioned before, where language traditions survive and die in a hodgepodge fashion, leaving behind a patchwork of inconsistencies and weirdness. Old spellings persist even though old pronunciations do not.

Another reason spelling is hard for some folks is that if you are an avid reader—and I hope you are, as it is a great way to improve your language—you will pick up the peculiarities and habits of those authors. Even if you did, at one point, spell a word in what is considered correct for your place and time, you might pick up a spelling that is more appropriate for some other place and time.

For example, in high school I read a great deal of Charles Dickens. I picked up the spelling *divers*, which is now considered an archaism for *diverse*. It took only one red mark on a school essay to drop that spelling very quickly!

4.2.1 BRITISH SPELLING VERSUS AMERICAN SPELLING

The differences between British and American spellings can be complicated, but the best advice I can give is to use the spelling your audience knows. It's a common myth that British English is the proper version; in fact, both varieties of English have changed substantially since 1776 but in different ways. Don't assume one is superior to the other in all situations.

For example, when I wrote a regular column about language for the *Malaysia Star*, I used spellings that would seem unusual to Americans, because Malaysia tends to follow the British way of spelling.

By the way, even the British don't always spell things the "British" way, and Canadians and Australians each have their own hybrid spelling that is neither completely British nor American.

Be on the lookout for these commonly confused British versus American spellings in your writing:

British	American
aeroplane	airplane
calibre	caliber
centre	center
colour	color
defence	defense
honour	honor
litre	liter
neighbour	neighbor
traveller	traveler

Keep in mind these are spelling variants. Neither word in each pair is the one true correct choice in all situations; they are perfectly acceptable variants that both have a home in English. Like so much with language, context matters. Use the spelling that fits the place and audience.

Also, don't worry about these particular spelling differences too much. For one thing, everyone will still understand what you mean if you use the wrong spelling. The spelling variants are mostly just one letter different.

For another, if you're worried about slipping up and spelling the word as you learned it in your home country instead of in the country you're visiting or studying in, just ask the locals, "How do you spell defence here?"

4.2.2 HOMOPHONE SPELLING ERRORS

Homophones are words that sound alike but are spelled differently. They are a common source of spelling mistakes. The best way to know which spelling is the correct one is to know what each word means, which can be inferred from seeing how others use it.

- **accept:** She *accepted* the award for best director.
- **except:** All my camping gear is packed *except* for my tent.

- **affect:** The lack of rain *affects* the tomato plants.
- **effect:** The bug spray had no *effect* on the mosquitoes.

- **close:** *Close* the door when you leave.
- **clothes:** There are clean *clothes* in the closet.

- **desert:** Never *desert* your friends when hiking.
- **dessert:** For *dessert*, we have key lime pie with homemade crust.

- **discreet:** Please be *discreet*—don't share this news with anyone else.
- **discrete:** These funds are *discrete* from the money we use to pay bills. The graphics are handled by a *discrete* processor.

- **ensure:** How can you *ensure* you'll be safe on your own?
- **insure:** If you *insure* your car, you will be protected in the event it is stolen.

- **it's:** *It's* time to leave. Whether *it's* fun or not, *it's* still a bad idea. *It's* been too long.
- **its:** She said *its* satellite had malfunctioned. The house lost *its* electricity.

- **lead:** Tests can determine whether there is *lead* in the water.
- **led:** Mother Cat *led* her kittens to the woods. He *led* a long and happy life.

- **passed:** No child *passed* the shop without looking at the toys in the window.
- **past:** In the *past*, we would have farmed our own food.

- **principal:** The school's *principal* retired after 40 years. The investment *principal* generated thousands in interest payments each year. The *principal* city of Ghana is Accra.
- **principle:** Our company's first *principle* is to treat everyone fairly. Following the scientific method is one of the *principles* of good research.

- **than:** His hair is curlier *than* hers. I'd rather walk *than* drive. I feel better today *than* I did yesterday.
- **then:** First stir the dry ingredients, *then* add the milk. If you really want to visit Mexico City, *then* what are you waiting for? We lived *then* in a tiny apartment in New York City.

- **their:** Children have *their* own ideas, just as adults do. They left *their* backpacks in class.
- **there:** *There* are a lot of farmers' markets in Paris. I went *there* to meet a friend. *There's* no way we can afford a house this big.

- **they're:** The muffins will be golden brown when *they're* done. Dogs show *they're* ready to play with wagging tails and playful poses.

- **to:** Go *to* the store. I need *to* find pants that fit. She has a right *to* know the truth.
- **too:** That's *too* much syrup! We were *too* tired to go to the after-party. Are you coming with us, *too*?
- **two:** There are *two* sides to every coin.

- **you're:** *You're* the kind of person we want to hire. Whether *you're* rich or poor, you still need to eat.
- **your:** *Your* responsibility is to make sure the dog does not escape. Where is *your* house? I noticed *your* swimming has improved.

4.3 Common Spelling Rules

Even though English spelling is inconsistent, we don't have to throw our hands in the air and say, "It's too hard! It can't be learned!" In fact, a few general rules apply to enough situations that they may be worth learning.

4.3.1 / BEFORE *E*

You may have heard the spelling guideline, "*I* before *E* except after *C*." However, many words don't follow this rule: *weird, their, height,* and so on. In fact, a careful analysis of English shows that "*I* before *E*" is only barely better advice than no rule at all: there are just too many exceptions.

You can improve upon the rule a little bit with this:

- *I* before *E* except after *C*,
  Or when sounded as "a"
  As in *neighbor* or *weigh*.

But a lot of *IE/EI* words don't conform to that rhyme, either. (Case in point: *either*.) There are even more versions of the rhyme, each trying to include a different group of exceptions, but not one covers the whole problem.

My advice is: Don't use any "*I* before *E*" rhyme. Instead, memorize those *IE* or *EI* words that give you the most trouble.

4.3.2 ADDING A SUFFIX AND DROPPING THE *E*

For root words that end in -*e*, drop that -*e* when you attach a word ending that begins with a vowel.

- change → changing
- gauge → gauging
- ice → icy

- love → loving
- rate → rating
- ride → riding

However, leave the final -*e* when you add a word ending that begins with a consonant.

- change → changes, changed, changer
- gauge → gauges, gauged
- ice → ices, iced

- love → loves, lovely, lover
- rate → rates, rated
- ride → rides, rider

Exceptions: words that end in *-ee, -oe,* or *-ye*:

- agree → agreeing
- canoe → canoeing
- dye → dyeing
- eye → eyeing
- hoe → hoeing
- see → seeing
- tiptoe → tiptoeing

Other exceptions:

- be → being
- notice → noticeable
- replace → replaceable
- see → seeing
- true → truly

Some words have more than one *-able* form:

- like → likeable, likable
- love → loveable, lovable
- move → moveable, movable

4.3.3 ADDING SUFFIXES TO WORDS ENDING IN *Y*

Change the *-y* to an *-i-* when you add a suffix, unless the suffix already begins with an *i*.

- defy → defies, defied, defiance, defying
- copy → copies, copied, copying
- occupy → occupies, occupied, occupying
- party → parties, partied, partying
- try → tries, tried, trying

4.3.4 DOUBLE THE FINAL CONSONANT WHEN ADDING SUFFIXES

When adding a suffix to a root word of a single syllable that contains a single vowel and ends with a single consonant, the final consonant is usually doubled.

- bat → batted, batting, batter
- grab → grabbed, grabber, grabbing
- stop → stopped, stopping, stopper

4.4 Affixes

Affixes are semantic elements that can be added to a word to change its meaning. *Prefixes* go before, *suffixes* go after, and *infixes* go in the middle. They change the meaning of the word or root to which they are attached.

4.4.1 INFLECTED ENDINGS

An **inflected ending** is a type of suffix that modifies (1) the *tense* of a verb to indicate the time, duration, completeness, quantity, or other quality of what is being referred to or (2) the *number*. These inflected endings come—of course, because this is English—with irregular as well as regular patterns.

In general, the older a word is in English, the more likely it is to be irregular, because, as mentioned in section 4.0, Spelling and Formatting, English has changed quite a bit, but some weird old forms still hang around.

See more in section 6.0, Verbs.

4.4.2 DERIVATIONAL SUFFIXES

Suffixes such as *-able*, *-ant*, *-ly*, *-ness*, *-ology*, and *-ure* can change a word from one part of speech to another. They are known as **derivational suffixes**. This is a completely ordinary way to make new words in English (part of its morphological vigor), and yet this kind of word transformation needlessly makes some English speakers uneasy, as if a great gaffe is being committed. It isn't.

This is another place where the history of English means that different suffixes that affect meaning in the same way are used with different roots and cannot be interchanged. For example, *-ic*, *-al*, and *-y* can all turn nouns into adjectives that mean "like [whatever the root is]," but *hero* becomes *heroic* and not *heroal* or *heroy*.

4.4.3 INFIXES

Infixes, which go in the middle of words, are rare in English, and the ones that do exist tend to be informal or profane. They are usually reserved for extreme emphasis. Here are some of the tamer ones:

- absolutely + bloody = abso-bloody-lutely (mildly offensive in the UK)
- absolutely + bleeding (a euphemized form of *bloody*) = abso-bleeding-lutely (mildly offensive in the UK)
- absolutely + blooming = abso-blooming-lutely
- absolutely + fricking (euphemism of an offensive word) = abso-fricking-lutely

- absolutely + posi(tive) = abso-posi-lutely
- fantastic + fricking = fan-fricking-tastic
- guaranteed + damn = guaran-damn-teed

4.4.4 COMMON PREFIXES

Prefixes go before a word.

PREFIX	MEANING	EXAMPLE
ab-	away, from	absent, abnormal
anti-	against	antifreeze, anticlimax
de-	opposite of	destruct, devalue
dis-	not, opposite of	disagree, discover
en-, em-	cause to	enact, encode, embrace
fore-	before, in front of	forecast, foretell
in-, im-	in, into	income, infield, imprint
in-, im-, il-, ir-	not	injustice, immoral, illegal, irrational
inter-	between, among	interact, interrupt
mid-	middle	midlife, midway
mis-	wrongly	misfire, misspell
non-	not	nonsense, nonviolent
over-	above, too much	overeat, overlook
pre-	before	prefix, preview
re-	again	return, rewrite
semi-	half, partly	semicircle, semifinal
sub-	under	submarine, subway
super-	above, beyond	superhuman, superstar
tele-	far	telephone, telescope
trans-	across, beyond, through	transmit, trans-oceanic, transport
un-	not, opposite of	unfriendly, unheard, unusual
under-	under, too little	underestimate, undercount, undersea

4.4.5 COMMON SUFFIXES

Suffixes go after a word.

SUFFIX	MEANING	EXAMPLE
-able, -ible	is, can be done	affordable, comfortable, likable, divisible
-al, -ial	having characteristics of	personal, universal, facial
-ed	past-tense verbs, adjectives	she rested, a painted door
-en	made of	golden, wooden
-er	comparative, more	higher, taller, weaker
-er, -or	one who does	speaker, worker, actor, tailor
-est	comparative, most	biggest, mildest, wickedest
-ful	full of	careful, helpful, mouthful
-ic	having characteristics of	elastic, linguistic, poetic
-ing	verb form, present participle	bringing, reading, running, sleeping
-ion, -tion, -ation, -ition	act, process	attraction, edition, reaction
-ity, -ty	state of	activity, infinity, society
-ive, -ative, -itive	adjective form of a noun	active, sensitive, talkative
-less	without	careless, fearless, hopeless
-ly	characteristic of, manner of	gratefully, kindly, lovely, quickly
-ment	state of, act of	contentment, enjoyment, resentment
-ness	state of, condition of	boldness, coldness, kindness
-ous, -eous, -ious	possessing the qualities of	joyous, courageous, gracious
-s, -es	more than one	books, girls, temples, churches
-y	characterized by	bubbly, happy, shiny

4.5 Contractions

Contractions are words made by combining other words and replacing some of the letters with an apostrophe ('). Most contractions are idiomatic, meaning their forms are fixed even if they don't seem to make sense to the modern English user. For example:

- will not = won't

Remember when we said English has a lot of baggage from its long history? *Won't* is actually a contraction of *woll not*, a much older form dating to at least as early as the mid-1500s.

Some teachers and reference works insist you should avoid contractions because they are deemed too informal or slangy. However, that is an insupportable view. Even the most respected and highly educated writers, thinkers, and leaders of our era regularly use contractions in a wide variety of writing and speaking, both formal and informal. In fact, if you try to avoid contractions, your writing and speech will come out sounding stilted and unnatural.

That said, it is also easy to overuse contractions in writing. A sentence like

- He didn't say he wouldn't've been ready if it weren't for the snow.

is a monstrosity that will make your readers' eyes pop out of their heads.

4.5.1 *IT'S* AND *IT'D*

It's and *It'd* are special contractions because each can be forms of different sets of words.

- it's = it has, it is
- it'd = it had, it would

4.5.2 OLD-FASHIONED CONTRACTIONS

The following contractions are considered old-fashioned today and should be avoided in everyday writing and speech. *'Tis*, in particular, is frequently misused and overused, especially by newspaper headline-writers at Christmas time.

- 'tis = it is
- 'twas = it was
- 'twere = it were
- 'twill = it will
- 'twould = it would

4.5.3 *Y'ALL*

Y'all, a contraction of *you all*, is widely used in informal conversation by millions of people, especially throughout the southern United States.

It's a second-person plural pronoun, which means it's used to refer directly to a group of people that may contain both men and women:

- Y'all should bring your swimsuits when you come to visit.

While *y'all* is a perfectly legitimate word, it should be avoided in formal writing and speech. Instead, use *you* or *you all*. Despite it seeming odd, *you* is the form for both the singular and plural second-person pronoun. See more in section 10.0, Pronouns.

4.5.4 *LET'S* IS A CONTRACTION FOR "LET US"

If you're using a form of the verb *to let*, meaning "to allow," the word will never have an apostrophe. If you're unsure whether you're using the right form, replace *let's* or *lets* with "let us" to see if the sentence makes sense.

- **Wrong:** She let's him play with the dog. Lets not forget why we agreed to help.
- **Right:** This gauge lets me see the temperature. Let's go to the movies.

4.6 Proper Nouns that End in *S*

We use the same *-'s* to form the possessive of proper nouns (names; see section 8.7) as we do for other nouns. Where it gets tricky is with names that already end in *-s*.

There are a few guidelines that can help you decide how to make the name possessive.

- If you say the possessive version of the name as "sez" or "zes" at the end, as with *charlezez* for *Charles*, then use *'s*: *Charles's*. Don't spell it *Charleses*.
- If the name sounds as if it already has an "es" or "eez" sound at the end, and ends in an *-s*, like *Bridges*, *Mercedes*, or *Moses*, then just use

an apostrophe: *Bridges'*, *Mercedes'*, *Moses'*. Note that *Reese's*, the candy maker, ends in an *e*, so it gets the *-'s* at the end, regardless of how it sounds.

- Certain ancient names traditionally take only an apostrophe, at least in formal works: *Achilles'*, *Euripides'*, *Jesus'*, *Venus'*, *Zeus'*. However, this tradition is weakening.

The overall trend in English is moving toward using *-'s* in most cases for making proper nouns possessive. Partly this is because many people feel the apostrophe hanging on the end of a word like *Sophocles'* just looks wrong. Some major style guides now permit, or even prefer, formations such as *Ganges's*, with the understanding that most speakers will not pronounce the second *s*.

However, I encourage you to be a little conservative on this. If you're writing for work or for school, use the same option that your institution or profession prefers, or that your boss or teacher uses, regardless of the preceding guidelines.

See also section 8.6.7 on the question of plural family names and section 8.6.1, Plurals of Some Greek and Latin Words.

4.7 Common Possessive Mistakes to Avoid

An apostrophe never makes a word plural. It either makes it possessive or shows it's a contraction.

- **Wrong:** Our grandparent's are visiting us during vacation.
- **Right:** I learned dozens of relatives' names at the family reunion.

The possessive apostrophe on a word made plural with -*s* never goes between a vowel and the -*s*.

- **Wrong:** ladie's night
- **Right:** ladies' night

Possessive pronouns (see section 10.0, Pronouns) never take an apostrophe.

- hers
- his
- its
- ours

- theirs
- whose
- yours

4.7.1 *ITS* VERSUS *IT'S*

Its versus *it's* is a confusing possessive pronoun, because it looks so much like the contraction *it's*.

The best way to decide which word to use is to ask yourself, if I replace *its/it's* with "it is" or "it has," does the sentence still make sense? If so, then use *it's*. If not, then use *its*.

- **Wrong:** dog can't catch it's tail.
- **Right:** It's a long way to Tipperary. It's been a pleasure speaking with you.

4.8 Dates

In the United States, dates are formatted a little differently than in the rest of the world. Typically, the United States puts it as *month-day-year*, like so:

- July 4, 1776, or 7/4/1776
- March 19, 2007, or 3/19/2007
- May 17, 1954, or 5/17/1954

In the rest of the world, you are far more likely to see basic dates written as *day-month-year*:

- 4 July 1776, or 4/7/1776
- 19 March 2007, or 19/3/2007
- 17 May 1954, or 17/5/1954

If you regularly encounter both ways of writing the date, it's easy to get frustrated, especially in cases where it's not clear from the context which system is being used. Does 6/5/1947 mean June 5, 1947, or May 6, 1947? Ask if you're not sure!

There is also a more functional standard used worldwide for technical and data-sharing purposes: *year-month-day*: *1957-06-05*.

In the spelled-out US form that uses the names of the months, such as *July 4, 1776*, notice the commas after the day and the year. That's an important style point easily overlooked.

- **Wrong:** Elvis Presley died August 16, 1977 at this home in Graceland. December 14 1972 was the last human spaceflight to the moon.
- **Right:** On December 17, 1903, the Wright brothers made the first powered airplane flight.

There's yet another way to write dates. You're likely to find it in formal or old-fashioned writing, or in government documents that adhere to old style rules. This uses *ordinal* numbers (see section

4.9, Numbers), such as first, twelfth, nineteenth, thirty-first, and so on.

- We proclaim the thirtieth of March as Marvin Hecshler Day in the City of Wooster, Ohio.
- The Fourth of July is a bank holiday in the United States.

However, do not use ordinal numbers with full dates.

- **Bad:** I think he was born on July 30th, 1970.
- **Good:** I think he was born on July 30, 1970.

The use of *on* is optional before the date (as in the example above). It may sound better to you with it. More formal writing (and most copyeditors) omit it.

4.8.1 DATE ABBREVIATIONS

The standard **abbreviations** for the months and days are:

- January: Jan.
- February: Feb.
- March: Mar. or not abbreviated
- April: Apr. or not abbreviated
- May: not abbreviated
- June: Jun. or not abbreviated
- July: Jul. or not abbreviated
- August: Aug.
- September: Sept.
- October: Oct.
- November: Nov.
- December: Dec.
- Monday: Mon.
- Tuesday: Tues. or Tue.
- Wednesday: Wed.
- Thursday: Thurs. or Thur.
- Friday: Fri.
- Saturday: Sat.
- Sunday: Sun.

For formal writing, always spell out the months and days. For informal writing, just be sure whichever style you choose is consistent and your readers will understand it.

4.8.2 DECADES AND YEARS CAN BE ABBREVIATED IN INFORMAL SITUATIONS

- '76 = 1776
- '04 = 1904
- the '80s = the 80s = the 1980s = the Eighties = the eighties

When the 2000s came around, most people did not abbreviate the years 2001–2009 as they did 1901–1909. So '04 almost always means 1904, '09 usually means 1909, and so forth.

There are competing styles for abbreviating a decade as a two-digit number, one with an apostrophe at the beginning and one without. Just as with contractions (see section 4.5), an apostrophe shows where letters—or, in this case, numbers—have been dropped.

- the '60s
- the 60s

Microsoft Word, the most widely used word processing software in the world, has for more than 30 years mistakenly autocorrected apostrophes at the beginning of words, including date abbreviations. The apostrophe should curve to the left, not the right.

- **Wrong:** the '80s
- **Right:** the '80s

4.8.3 TIME AND THE CLOCK

In North American English we use a.m. (*ante meridiem*, meaning "before midday") for the hours of the day between midnight (12 a.m.) and noon (12 p.m.), and p.m. (*post meridiem*, meaning "after midday") for the hours between noon and midnight. The abbreviations can be written several ways, varying capitalization, punctuation, and spacing. As always when you have choices, try to find out what your boss or teacher prefers and stick to it.

- 2 A.M.—2 a.m.—2 am—2am
- 5:30 P.M.—5:30 p.m.—5:30 pm—5:30pm

Note that in Europe and other parts of the world, it is common to use a 24-hour clock (what people in the United States tend to think of as military time). With a 24-hour clock, the hours don't start over after noon but continue increasing until resetting to zero at midnight.

- 12:00 a.m. = "midnight" = 00:00
- 1:00 a.m. = 0100 = "oh one hundred hours" = "one in the morning"
- 7:10 a.m. = 7:10 = 0710 = "seven ten" = "seven ten in the morning"
- 12:00 p.m. = "noon" = 12:00
- 1:00 p.m. = 13:00 = 1300 = "thirteen hundred hours" = "one in the afternoon"
- 6:20 p.m. = 18:20 = 1820 = "eighteen twenty" = "six twenty at night"

It's usually clearer to use *midnight* and *noon* instead of 12:00 a.m. and 12:00 p.m.

Even with the dominance of digital clocks, which have no spinning second, minute, or hour hands, we still keep using the old ways of talking about time derived from clocks with dials and faces.

One old-fashioned way of telling time that has hung on for almost 500 years is *o'clock*, a contraction of *of the clock*. It is used only when the time is exactly on the hour.

- 9 a.m. = 9 o'clock in the morning
- 11:00 p.m. = 11 o'clock at night

We don't use *o'clock* if there are minutes after the hour in the time.

- **Wrong:** 9:10 o'clock

The halfway mark in an hour also has its own terminology.

- 7:30 = "seven-thirty" = "half past seven" = "half seven" (mostly in the UK)

We also use quarter-hours in English time-telling, especially when estimating time. A quarter hour is 15 minutes, which is one-quarter of the hour's 60 minutes.

- 9:15 = "nine fifteen" = "a quarter past nine"
- 10:45 = "a quarter before eleven" = "a quarter to eleven" = "a quarter of eleven"

For all other times, we use similar constructions:

- 2:55 = "two fifty-five" = "five minutes before three" = "five minutes to three" = "five of three"

Since we often give approximate times in English, sometimes we want to emphasize that we are talking about very specific times.

- The meeting starts at 3 p.m. *on the dot*.
- You'll miss the train if you're not there at 6:20 *sharp*.

Time can be both a non-count noun and a count noun (see section 8.4).

- He called her five times.
- How many times did you run around the track?
- I need more time to finish my homework.
- It's about time to leave.

4.8.4 IDIOMATIC TIME MEASUREMENTS

There are several idiomatic expressions involving time that may be easy for English language learners to confuse.

Five minutes and *15 minutes* are often used as casual time estimates rather than exact measures, especially in the spoken language.

- I was only outside for *five minutes* and the rain soaked me. = I was outside for a short period of time, probably more than one minute, but probably less than ten minutes.

- We'll be there in *15 minutes*. = We'll be there in more than five minutes but less than 30 minutes.

On time means something is happening when it is supposed to.

- We were *on time* for the meeting. = We were there when the meeting started.
- The bus was *on time*. = The bus arrived when it was supposed to.

In time means something happens, happened, or could happen, without being late. We usually follow *in time* with a verb. Frequently, it appears with *just*, as in *just in time*, which indicates that whatever it was, it happened with almost no extra time to spare.

- Will the hero arrive *in time* to stop the villain? = Will the hero arrive soon enough to be able to stop the villain?
- We arrived *just in time* for the movie. = We arrived right before the movie started.

The time, with the definite article *the*, is used to refer to events that have happened, but without being specific about when.

- Do you remember *the time* we swam across the river?
- Then there was *the time* you wore pajamas to school.

One time is often used to introduce a story about something specific that happened, without being specific about when.

- *One time* at band camp we put a frog in the director's bed.
- *One time* I did my hair like my mother did hers when she was a girl.

Once upon a time is a formal way of introducing a story, especially a fairy tale or folk tale.

- *Once upon a time* there was a princess who lived in an enchanted palace in a mighty city.

4.9 Numbers

There are two main types of numbers in English: **cardinal** and **ordinal**.

Cardinal numbers are used most of the time, whether you're speaking or writing. They are the *counting numbers*. They express both positive and negative values.

- We'll need about 30 boxes to pack up all the books.
- Fifty years ago, we found this amulet in a mountain cave.
- The wind chill makes it feel like minus 20 degrees outside.

Ordinal numbers usually show the order or sequence of things, such as rankings or dates. They differ in their usage and their word endings.

- I was used to the odd hours by the second month of working the late shift.
- Sometime after October 10th, we're going camping in the mountains.

Cardinal	Ordinal
1: one	1st: first
2: two	2nd: second

3: three	3rd: third
4: four	4th: fourth
5: five	5th: fifth
6: six	6th: sixth
7: seven	7th: seventh
8: eight	8th: eighth
9: nine	9th: ninth
10: ten	10th: tenth
11: eleven	11th: eleventh
12: twelve	12th: twelfth
13: thirteen	13th: thirteenth
14: fourteen	14th: fourteenth
15: fifteen	15th: fifteenth
20: twenty	10th: twentieth
37: thirty-seven	37th: thirty-seventh
80: eighty	80th: eightieth
100: one hundred	100th: one hundredth

Sometimes people will use the quasi-ordinal *nth*. The *n* stands for an unknown number.

- For the *nth* time, do not jump on the couch!
- This car is perfectly engineered to the *nth* degree.

4.9.1 PARTIAL NUMBERS

There are two main kinds of partial numbers: *fractions* and *decimals*. Which you use depends on the circumstances.

Fractions are common in recipes, where traditional measurements such as ¼ *cup* or ½ *teaspoon* are likely to appear. Fractions are also far more common than decimals in casual conversation, particularly when a quantity is unknown or estimated. In prose, we usually write out the fractions in words and use hyphens to separate the numerals and the words. They are represented as numerals in mathematics, recipes, and formulas.

- We spent nine-tenths of our time on the trip arguing about the map.
- Surveys show that something like a third of all citizens are trying to conserve water.
- Blend ¾ cup sugar, ½ cup buttermilk, and ½ teaspoon salt.
- Start with 1½ cups of flour.
- My phone's battery lasts only two-thirds of the day.
- Half of all people will experience a temporary disability.

Decimals tend to be used for precise measurements in scientific, financial, and academic fields.

- 0.65 liters
- 3.14159 inches
- 400.03 points

In decimals, if there are no numerals in front of the decimal point, put a zero. It makes it easier to notice the decimal.

- **OK:** .44
- **Better:** 0.44

4.9.2 WRITING NUMBERS

In most writing, such as for school or work, the numbers zero through nine should be written out as words rather than as numerals. Numbers 10 and higher should be written as numerals, except when they begin a sentence (see section 4.9.4).

- There are three cookies left in the jar.
- He has zero chances at winning the race, but he won't stop trying.
- For more than 100 years, my family has made the best olive oil in Italy.
- The team gave me a jersey with the number 19 on it.
- Twenty-three pairs of shoes were left near the door.

If you have a series of numbers, they should all be in the same style, even if some are below and some are above 10.

- **Bad:** My siblings are eight, 10, and 12 years old.
- **Good:** My siblings are eight, ten, and twelve years old.

In literary writing, it can be less distracting to the reader to see all numbers as words, and it's often better to use general rather than specific numbers. There is something about the exactness of numbers that can destroy the mood of an emotional bit of writing.

- **Good:** I scooted over a few inches on the bench until we could hold hands.
- **Not Good:** I scooted over four inches on the bench until we could hold hands.
- **Even Less Good:** I scooted over 4 inches on the bench until we could hold hands.

In the United States, bank checks are still popular. These checks usually have the numbers written out two ways: once in numerals and once in words. This makes sure banks know exactly how much money to move from the check writer's account to the check recipient's account. For the sake of readability, it is best to separate each grouping of numbers with commas and to use "and" for the cents.

- $601 = six hundred one dollars
- $1,515,657 = one million, five hundred fifteen thousand, six hundred fifty-seven dollars
- $2999.04 = two thousand, nine hundred ninety-nine dollars, and four cents

For writing dates, see section 4.8.

4.9.3 PERCENTAGES AS NUMBERS

Percentages are best written as numbers, except, as noted in section 4.9.4, when they begin a sentence.

- Up to 90 percent of school kids say they would rather choose their own teachers.

4.9.4 NUMBERS THAT START SENTENCES

Numbers at the beginning of sentences should always be written as words, even if they are above nine.

If it looks too awkward, then rewrite the sentence so the number doesn't start things off.

- Ninety minutes into the movie the baby started crying.
- Ten days ago, I had the best key lime pie of my life.
- **Bad:** Nine thousand, four hundred seven dollars would pay off my mortgage.
- **Good:** My mortgage would be paid off with $9,407.

4.9.5 PLACE PUNCTUATION IN NUMBERS

There are two styles of writing numbers that are four digits long to the left of the decimal: with or without a comma after the "thousands" place. Either is fine, but be consistent.

- 2342 = 2,342
- 1132 = 1,132

Most of the English-speaking world uses commas to set off the places in long numbers, but in some countries in Europe and South America, periods are more common, and then a comma is used where North Americans would use a decimal. As always, it's important to know your audience when writing.

- 8,851,080.11 in North America = 8.851.080,11 in parts of Europe and South America
- 21,163,226.40 in North America = 21.163.226,40 in parts of Europe and South America

4.9.6 SAYING NUMBERS AS WORDS

- 1,000, thousands: say "thousand": "one thousand," "nine thousand"
- 100, hundreds: say "hundred": "one hundred," "four hundred"

- 10, tens: say just the number: "ten," "twenty"
- 1, ones: say just the number: "one," "six"
- 0.1, tenths: say as singular or plural: "one tenth," "two tenths"
- 0.01, hundredths: say as singular or plural: "one hundredth," "eight hundredths"
- 0.001, thousandths: say as singular or plural: "one thousandth," "four thousandths"
- 0.0001, ten-thousandths: say as singular or plural: "one ten-thousandth," "three ten-thousandths"

4.9.7 *ZERO* VERSUS *OH*

When reading numbers aloud in English, a zero is often said as "oh." It may seem confusing to give the name of the letter *O* to the number 0 when they look so much alike—though the oh is usually rounder and the zero narrower—but it's usually clear from the situation which one is correct. Where you're most likely to encounter difficulty is with serial numbers, passwords, or other randomized numbers.

- (212) 555-1204 = "two one two, five five five, one two oh four"
- 4.0 = "four point oh"
- s304fozv = "ess three zero four eff oh zee vee"

4.9.8 SAYING PHONE NUMBERS

Unlike other countries, in the United States people tend to say phone numbers as a series of single digits and not groupings of two or three digits, as shown in section 4.9.7. However, especially for businesses, this is not always the case.

- 1 (800) 555-8262 = one, eight hundred, five five five, eighty-two sixty-two
- (212) 555-1010 = two one two, five five five, ten ten

4.9.9 WRITING AMOUNTS OF MONEY

Money isn't very different from the previous guidelines (section 4.9, Numbers), but there are a few places where you need to be alert to common mistakes.

- Avoid indicating "dollars" or "cents" twice:
  - ▸ **Wrong:** $1.2 million dollars, $0.30 cents, 0.30¢
  - ▸ **Right:** $1.2 million, $0.30, 30 cents.

The word *money* is almost never plural in everyday English. Only in the most technical financial situations, such as when discussing a corporation's or a government's budget, is it used. For nearly all uses for most people, it should be just *money*, even if you're talking about more than one source or kind of money.

- **Bad:** How many *monies* do you have? Lend me five bucks.
- **Good:** How much *money* do you have? Lend me five bucks.

5.0

SENTENCE
STRUCTURE

STRUCTURE

Although they come in a variety of lengths and forms, sentences tend to be made of just a few basic features. Understanding these features will help you when writing is difficult.

The basic parts of every sentence are *subjects*, *predicates*, *objects*, and *clauses*. They can appear in many different forms and places.

5.1 Subjects and Predicates

The **subject** of a sentence is the main actor of the sentence: the person, animal, or thing performing the verb.

The **predicate** of a sentence is what is being done. It's the verb and everything connected to the verb, including whatever the verb is acting on. A predicate always keeps company with a subject, and it has a voice (see section 6.6) and a tense (see section 6.4). In English, we usually put the subject before the predicate. Consider the following simple sentence:

- Miguel sells cars.

Here *Miguel* is the subject and *sells cars* is the predicate. When a sentence has both a subject and predicate, it is considered complete, as opposed to being a sentence fragment. In writing, most ordinary sentences are complete. However, sentence fragments are far more common when speaking. Where beginning writers often go astray is trying to transcribe fragments of spoken language exactly as they hear them.

5.2 Subject-Verb Agreement

The subject and verb in a sentence must agree in number. That is, if the subject is plural, the verb must be conjugated in the proper plural form. If the subject is singular, then the verb must be conjugated in the proper singular form. (See more at section 6.0, Verbs.)

- *Crows are* loud birds.
- The *little girl waves* to the bus driver.

However, for *either/or* and *neither/nor* sentences, the verb is conjugated based on the subject nearest to it.

- Either our dad or our *grandparents are* picking us up.
- Neither our grandparents nor our *dad is* picking us up.

A phrase or clause that comes between the subject and the verb does not change the antecedent's number.

- *Mexican food*, no matter what you think of hot peppers, *is* its own reward.

Compound subjects are matched with a plural referent.

- *An ambulance and a fire truck are* on their way to the scene of the accident.

When you use indefinite pronouns such as *anybody*, *each*, *everybody*, and *someone*, use a singular verb.

- *Each* of the voters *takes* a ballot.
- *Someone was speaking* out of turn.

For more on subject-verb agreement, see section 6.7, Conjugating Verbs.

5.3 Objects

Objects are what is acted upon or affected by the verb. There are three kinds of objects found in sentences: *direct objects*, *indirect objects*, and *objects of a preposition*.

A **direct object** is acted upon by the verb.

- Miguel sells cars.

Cars is the object, because it is what is being sold.

An **indirect object** receives or is acted upon by the direct object. We can revise our sentence to include an indirect object:

- Miguel sells businesses cars.

In this version of our sentence, *cars* is still the direct object, but it now has an indirect object, *businesses*.

The **object of a preposition** (see section 13.0, Prepositions) could be said to direct the action of the verb and tell us how the verb was performed. The object comes after the preposition. For example:

- Ani pushed the bicycle onto the sidewalk.

In this sentence, *the sidewalk* is the object of the preposition *onto*, and it tells us how *pushed* happened.

5.4 Clauses

If you have a phrase or sentence with a subject and a predicate, then you have a **clause**. The clause can be sophisticated or simple, but it's still a clause.

An **independent clause** can function on its own and looks much like a regular sentence.

- I left my backpack on the bus.

A **dependent clause** cannot function on its own because it leaves an idea or thought unfinished.

- when I left my backpack on the bus

That's a dependent clause because the word *when* leaves us wondering. It's perfectly fine to have a dependent clause, but it should always keep company with other clauses that complete them, like this:

- When I left my backpack on the bus, the driver gave it back the next day.

Note that *the driver gave it back the next day* is not a dependent clause because, except for capitalizing "The," it could exist on its own as a sentence.

5.5 Subordinators

The *when* in *when I left my backpack on the bus* is an example of a **subordinator**, which introduces a dependent clause.

Subordinators do the work of connecting the dependent clause to another clause to complete the sentence. In each of these examples, the first word is a subordinator:

- because her old hat had lost its shape
- that was in the cupboard behind the cans
- which he bought as soon as it was on the market

Subordinators can include relative pronouns (see section 10.6), subordinating conjunctions (see section 14.3), and noun clause markers.

Noun clause markers are useful when you want to connect two independent clauses. They include:

- how
- however
- if
- that
- what
- whatever
- when
- whenever
- where
- wherever
- whether
- which
- whichever
- who
- whoever
- whom
- whomever
- whose
- why

▸ Willa learned. + The horses are tame enough to ride. = Willa learned that the horses are tame enough to ride.
▸ I can't understand. + What is he saying? = I can't understand what he is saying.

▸ Sunil wonders. + Can the Mets win the World Series? = Sunil wonders whether the Mets can win the World Series.

That is a special noun clause marker that can be omitted. The others cannot. For example:

▪ Willa learned that the horses are tame enough to ride. = Willa learned the horses are tame enough to ride.

In fact, many copyeditors and professors will insist that you remove *thats* like that as being unnecessary.

5.6 Phrases

While a clause has both a subject and a predicate, a **phrase** does not. A phrase can simply be a cohesive set of words that makes some sense. Phrases are usually parts of clauses, and they can function as a part of speech, such as a *verb phrase* (see section 5.6.2), *noun phrase* (see section 5.6.1), or *prepositional phrase* (see section 5.6.3).

Phrase	**Clause**
yogurt in the smoothie	I put yogurt in the smoothie.
broken window	A broken window lets the cold in.
because of the high cost	because it costs a lot
after the concert	after the concert ends

5.6.1 NOUN PHRASES

A noun phrase works as a single noun-like unit even though it may contain more than one word.

Noun phrases start with nouns and pronouns, to which adjectives, verbs, determiners, and other parts of speech are added.

- *People who have cars* spend less time walking.
- We found the source of *the water leaking into the closet*.

One type of noun phrase is an *appositive phrase*, where the subject is defined or restated, usually right after it.

- Guthrie, *my son*, imagines going to space.
- My son *Guthrie* imagines going to space.

In the first sentence, the aside set off by commas adds a bit of nonessential information about Guthrie. In the second sentence, we are naming him, as I have more than one son and it is a way of specifying which son I mean.

Another type of noun phrase is a *gerund phrase*, which is made from a verb but behaves like a noun.

- *Running* is the only exercise I enjoy.

There are also *infinitive phrases*, which use an unconjugated form of the verb.

- I love *to run* before dawn.

5.6.2 VERB PHRASES

Verb phrases start with a verb and may include a direct or indirect object, or a complement (see section 5.7).

They do not include the subject. Verb phrases can sometimes behave like adjectives or adverbs.

- It *may be time* for new snow tires.
- The thunderstorm *would have awakened* anyone.
- We need a motion *to end this meeting*.

5.6.3 PREPOSITIONAL PHRASES

Prepositional phrases do not have a verb or a subject and, like noun phrases and verb phrases, function as a unit.

They contain a preposition and the object of the preposition (see section 13.0, Prepositions), with adjectives sometimes appearing between them. These phrases can act like adjectives and adverbs.

- The gold dress *with the shiny trim* looks blue.
- Our awareness *of our unconscious minds* is weak.
- As the train climbed *through the snowy Swiss Alps*, I felt cozy *in my berth*.

5.6.4 ABSOLUTE PHRASES

Absolute phrases modify the entire sentence and are set off by commas or dashes from it.

- *Our work finished*, we headed down to the pub.
- *The show over*, the cast and crew went to Sardi's for drinks.

5.7 Complements

A **complement** completes the predicate. It finishes the idea started by the subject or object or a verb.

A **subject complement** comes after a linking verb (see section 6.9) and describes or redefines the subject.

- Her dog is a beagle.—*Beagle* is the subject complement.
- You seem worried.—*Worried* is the subject complement.
- The caterpillar became a moth.—*Moth* is the subject complement.

An **object complement**, usually a noun or adjective or words behaving like one, refers to a direct object (see section 5.3, Objects).

- They painted the bike shed blue.—*Bike shed* is the direct object, and *blue* is the object complement.
- Customers called the product "unobtainium" and the name stuck.—*Product* is the direct object and *unobtainium* is the object complement.

A **verb complement** supplements the understanding of another verb. In other words, one verb is the object of the others. We do this three ways:

1. With noun clauses:
   ▶ He knew she had finished.—*She had finished* is the verb complement to *knew*.

2. With infinitives:

   ▶ I want to finish this.—*To finish* this is the verb complement
   to *want*.

3. With gerunds:

   ▶ I thought swimming in the dark would be fun.—*Swimming in the dark* is a verb complement to *thought*.

6.0

VERBS

WORDS

Verbs describe what we're doing, feeling, or thinking, or the state or condition of a thing, person, or animal. Verbs form or lead into the *predicate* (see section 5.1, Subjects and Predicates), the part of a sentence that tells us what the subject is doing.

6.1 Person

Person tells us about the relationship between the subject of the verb—the individual who is doing the verb—and the person who is being spoken to. The person of a verb is signaled by pronoun choice and verb endings.

First person means the speaker is also the subject. It's often used in novels, especially for narration. The pronouns *I, me, mine, my, we, our, ours*, and *us* are common in the first person.

- I plan to break in my new boots before the hiking trip.
- We are ready for our close-ups, Mr. DeMille.

Second person means the speaker is talking directly to someone who is probably present. Sometimes, this is a narrator speaking to the reader, but it's far more common in instructions, how-to guides, recipes, and advice. The pronouns *you* and *yours* are common in the second person.

- You should wear your hat.
- Why won't you listen to me?
- When you get to the end of the chapter, write the answers to the questions in your notebook.

Third person means the subject is not present and the speaker is not speaking directly to them. It's often used for relating stories about someone else. The pronouns *he, her, hers, him, his, it, its, she, them,* and *they* are common in the third person.

- She says she plans to donate her old car to charity.
- They won't know what the problem is until their computer technician takes a look.
- The rains in Spain fall mainly on the plain.

6.2 Number

Number tells us how many people make up the subject of the verb. We have either a singular subject (just one) or a plural subject (two or more).

Mass nouns, which act as a singular subject even though they refer to lots of things, take the singular conjugation.

- A flock of geese soars into the sky.
- The crowd wonders when the theater will open.

6.3 Aspect

Aspect tells you how long a verb's action happened. **Simple** actions are completed at an unknown time. **Progressive** actions continue. **Perfect** actions were known to be completed in the past. **Perfect progressive** actions were known to be continuous in the past.

6.4 Tense

Tense tells us when the verb of the sentence is taking place, from the point of view of the subject of the sentence.

To illustrate, let's use examples from the verbs *eat*, *call*, and *read*.

6.4.1 PAST TENSE

Simple past tense is for actions that happened at a specific time.

- I ate.
- I called.
- I read.

Past progressive is for actions that happened continuously but were interrupted.

- I was eating.
- I was calling.
- I was reading.

Past perfect is for actions that happened but were finished before a specific time. This was traditionally called the *pluperfect*.

- I had eaten.
- I had called.
- I had read.

Past perfect progressive is for actions that happened continuously but then stopped happening continuously at a specific time.

- I had been eating.
- I had been calling.
- I had been reading.

6.4.2 PRESENT TENSE

Simple present tense happens now and is repeated. It's about habits or regular events.

- I eat.
- I call.
- I read.

Present progressive actions are continuously happening now.

- I am eating.
- I am calling.
- I am reading.

Present perfect actions started and finished in the past at an unspecified time but are relevant to the present.

- I have eaten.
- I have called.
- I have read.

Present perfect progressive is for actions that were continuously happening in the past and are still happening now.

- I have been eating.
- I have been calling.
- I have been reading.

6.4.3 FUTURE TENSE

There are two forms that talk about the future. *Will* forms tend to be about a promise, intention, or voluntary action. *Going to* forms tend to be about plans or a certain future.

Simple future says that a specific event will happen at a specific time.

- I will eat. I am going to eat.
- I will call. I am going to call.
- I will read. I am going to read.

Future progressive says what will be happening continuously.

- I will be eating. I am going to be eating.
- I will be calling. I am going to be calling.
- I will be reading. I am going to be reading.

Future perfect says that at a certain future time, a specific event will have happened.

- I will have eaten. I am going to have eaten.
- I will have called. I am going to have called.
- I will have read. I am going to have read.

Future perfect progressive says that at a certain future time, a continuous event will have been happening.

- I will have been eating. I will have been going to eat.
- I will have been calling. I will have been going to call.
- I will have been reading. I will have been going to read.

6.5 Mood

Don't be misled into thinking **mood** is about emotions. Instead, it refers to whether or not something is a fact.

Indicative mood tells us things that are true. It is by far the most common.

Subjunctive mood suggests possibility, wishes, or hypotheticals, especially in contradiction to what is true.

The subjunctive has been on a long, slow decline in English. Where the subjunctive has traditionally been used, it is now often replaced by what appears to be the simple present or simple past. I say *appears*, because what we may be seeing is not the vanishing of the subjunctive, but instead a simplification of its forms. In other words, it still functions as the subjunctive, but it takes the same form as other tenses. For example, both of these sentences suggest a hypothetical situation, even though their verb forms are different.

- If you were to come with me, we could have lunch.
- If you came with me, we could have lunch.

Imperative mood makes a verb into a command. It uses the second person, even when, for example, the subject is speaking to herself or himself.

- Go get me a pair of pliers.
- "Get up and ride that horse again," I told myself. "Do it now."

6.6 Voice

The **voice** of a verb has nothing do with the sounds made by the mouth. Instead, it has to do with who or what is performing or doing the verb.

Active voice is used when the subject performs the verb and appears *in front* of the verb.

- She saved my life.
- Our team won the game.

Passive voice uses a different word order to put the direct object before the verb, and the subject after the verb.

- My life was saved by her.
- The game was won by us.

The words *passive* and *active* here are different from their non-linguistic meanings. Don't make the mistake of assuming that *active* is for bold, clear-thinking achievers, and *passive* is for wimpy, vague do-nothings. It isn't true.

Both *active* and *passive* voices are essential to everyday writing and speaking. Broadside suggestions that you should avoid the passive voice are misguided and should be ignored.

What you should try to avoid is using passive voice to deflect responsibility, unless that's what you're aiming for. "Mistakes were made by us," sounds much less like an admission of guilt than, "We made mistakes." The first one is passive; the latter is active. The first one deflects the blame a little bit (and, if it's in apology, may signal to others that you're not sincere), whereas the second one plainly claims the blame (and may signal sincerity).

Passive voice is rightly used when you can't or don't need to explicitly identify the subject. Perhaps the subject—the main actor—is unknown, or doesn't matter, or is understood from the context.

- An umbrella was left behind after the concert.
- The man was indicted on two counts of armed robbery.

The only other valid complaint about passive voice is that it makes readers and listeners work a little bit harder to understand what is being said. We can understand it, but the active voice may be a better way to write it. When you're revising your writing, try to write sentences in different ways to see which works best.

Some people have mistakenly been taught that forms of the verbs *to be* or *to have* usually indicate the passive voice. This is sometimes the case but is not a valid indicator of what is truly passive voice.

6.7 Conjugating Verbs

We change verbs to indicate who is talking and to whom (the person; see section 6.1) and to show when the verb happened (the tense; see section 6.4). This change is **conjugation**, which we do by adding inflections. What form the conjugation takes depends upon the person and tense of the verb.

There are three main regular ways to conjugate verbs: now, in the past, and as continuous action.

6.7.1 NOW

In this conjugation, primarily used for the present and future tenses, the ending is the same for the first-person, second-person, and third-person plural, but in the third-person singular, an -*s* is added. The *infinitive form* in English is this conjugation with *to* before it: *to eat, to swim, to live*, and so on.

This conjugation can also indicate the historical simple tense, which you may encounter in academic writing. In the present tense, a thing is happening while the words are being said, whereas in the *historical simple tense*, important past events are described as if they are happening right now, although it is usually clear from the context that there's no way they could be.

Present

- I eat vegetables. You grow vegetables. She prefers vegetables.

Historical Simple

- Columbus sails to the New World and hunts for gold.
- Einstein takes a job as an assistant professor in Zurich.

6.7.2 IN THE PAST

In this conjugation, we indicate that something happened in the past by adding -*ed* to most verbs. This creates the past participle, which is used in the past and perfect tenses.

- He wondered who would win. The ball stayed in bounds.
  She helped the coach.

  Words formed with this inflection often behave like adjectives and can modify other words.

- The finished sculpture is beautiful.
- A newly cleaned house looks nice.

6.7.3 CONTINUOUS ACTION

In this conjugation, we indicate that something is happening, or has happened, over a period of time. It is used in the present progressive tense and similar forms and is called the present participle.

- We are selling the house. He is trying to find a seat.
  She is standing in the hall.

  Words formed with this inflection sometime behave like an adjective.

- Falling water makes a pleasant sound.
- You have to feed growing children at least three times a day.
- A bleating calf finds its mother.

This conjugation also creates the **gerund** (section 5.6.1, Noun Phrases), a form of the verb that behaves like a noun.

- Knowing her has been a pleasure.
- Your smoking is bothering the other customers.
- Their laughing has nothing to do with you.

Note that if the gerund is preceded by a pronoun, the possessive form is the best choice.

- **Bad:** Him quitting left us without a center fielder.
- **Good:** His quitting left us without a center fielder.

6.8 Action Verbs

Action verbs indicate what the subject of a sentence is doing. In good writing, action verbs can make the reader feel emotions, see scenes more vividly, and accurately know what is happening. Action verbs can be *transitive* or *intransitive*.

Transitive verbs have a direct object, which is the thing or person being acted upon by the verb.

- Paint the car.—*Car* is the direct object.
- She folded the newspaper.—*Newspaper* is the direct object.
- Did you get a good grade?—*Good grade* is the direct object.
- We greeted him at the airport.—*Him* is the direct object.

Intransitive verbs do not act upon anything. They may be followed by an adjective, adverb, preposition, or another part of speech.

- She smiled, then left the party.
- Great crowds of people milled about the town square.
- I awaken every day in the same way.

6.9 Linking Verbs

Linking verbs add details about the subject of a sentence. In their simplest form, they connect the subject and the sentence complement—that is, the adjective, noun, or pronoun that follows the linking verb. They link them together instead of showing action. The linguistic term for this connection is *copula*.

Often, what is on each side of a linking verb is equivalent; the complement redefines or restates the subject.

- My car is a Renault.
- Our favorite food is kale.

Some verbs in the following list often act as linking verbs but can also be action verbs. To figure out if they are acting as linking verbs, try replacing them with forms of *to be*. If the changed sentence makes sense, you have replaced a linking verb. Here are some common linking verbs:

- act
- appear
- be
- become

- feel
- grow
- look
- prove
- remain
- seem
- smell
- sound
- stay
- taste
- turn

▸ She *appears* ready for the election. She *is* ready for the election.
▸ The food *seemed* spoiled. The food *was* spoiled.
▸ He *acted* surprised about the gift. He *was* surprised about the gift.
▸ You *look* exhausted. You *are* exhausted.

6.10 Auxiliary Verbs

Also called *helping verbs*, **auxiliary verbs** extend the main verb by helping to show time, tense, and possibility. The auxiliary verbs are *be*, *have*, and *do*. They are used in the continuous (progressive) and perfect tenses.

In the progressive tenses, the auxiliary verb *be* and its conjugated forms are part of the construction that shows that the action is or was happening continuously.

- We *are getting* ready to go.
- We *were swimming* for an hour when it started to rain.
- I *am feeling* kind of ill.
- She *was flipping* the pancakes high into the air.

In the perfect tenses, the auxiliary verb *have* and its conjugated forms are used to indicate a continuous action that is finished and to indicate actions that are continuously happening but have not finished yet.

- She *had rebuilt* the engine before race day.
- I *had been thinking* about doing that before you suggested it.
- *Have* you *been dating* him long?

Do is an especially common auxiliary verb that is used to ask questions, to express negation, to provide emphasis, and more.

Do is used for questions in the simple present and simple past.

- *Do* you have homework to finish?
- *Did* you finish your homework?
- *Doesn't* she have a cute baby?
- *Didn't* you see her cute baby?

Do is used for negations in the simple present and simple past tenses.

- We *don't* have football practice on Sundays.
- She *didn't* finish her broccoli.

Do is used in the negative imperative, which is when you tell someone not to do something.

- *Don't* get mud on the carpet.
- *Don't* leave the door open.

Do is used for emphasis, usually in a situation where there has been some doubt about the truth. If you were reading these sentences aloud, you would put a lot of emphasis on the form of *do*.

- She *does* run the company! She's the CEO.
- We *did* go to rehearsal, but the building was locked.

6.11 Modal Verbs

Modal verbs, also known as conditionals, are a kind of auxiliary verb. They assist the main verb in suggesting ability, possibility, potential, expectation, permission, and obligation. When used with the main verb, modal verbs do not end with *-s* for the third-person singular.

- can
- could
- may
- might
- must

- ought to
- shall
- should
- will
- would

- I *may* not *want* to see you again later.
- They *must give* their time to a worthy cause.
- She *should tell* him exactly how she feels.
- *Would* you *open* the door for me?

A characteristic of modals is that they are used in inverted forms when a statement becomes a question.

- We *can come* to the party. → *Can* we *come* to the party?
- He *will go* to the party. → *Will* he *go* to the party?

There are three verbs that behave like modals some of the time, but like main verbs the rest of the time: *dare, need to,* and *used to.*

As Modals

- Don't you *dare give* him more candy!
- I *need to drive* to the store.
- I *used to go* to that school.

As Main Verbs

- We *dare* not give them candy for breakfast.
- I *need* more money.
- I am *used to* the rattling my car makes.

6.11.1 MULTIPLE MODALS

Multiple modals are a dialect feature that uses two or more modals in a single sentence to emphasize possibility. While they are especially common in the Appalachian and Southern dialects of American English, they should be avoided in formal and academic speech and writing.

- I *might could* go with you if you'll let me get my coat.
- It *shouldn't ought* to rain today.

6.12 Irregular Verb Inflections

Irregular verbs are hangers-on from previous versions of English, from centuries ago. Generally, they show their Germanic roots, and they come from a time before spelling was as regularized as it is today. It would be impossible to make a full account of all the variations of irregularly inflected English verbs in a work of this brief scope, but you will find them fully detailed in most dictionaries.

The most common irregular verb in English is *to be*. This verb would normally cause problems for only the newest of English learners, but novice writers often make problems for themselves when they try to avoid forms of *to be* because they are so common. This leads to such offenses as

- There existed no more cereal in the cabinet.

instead of

- There was no more cereal in the cabinet.

The present participle of *to be* is *being* and the past participle is *been*.

The other two most common irregular verbs are *to have* (present participle: *having*, past participle: *had*) and *to do* (present participle: *doing*, past participle: *done*).

Following is a chart of other irregular verbs, with the most common at the top. I've included just their key irregular forms.

INFINITIVE	PAST TENSE	PAST PARTICIPLE
say	said	said
go	went	gone
take	took	taken
get	got	got/gotten
come	came	come
see	saw	seen
make	made	made
know	knew	known
give	gave	given
find	found	found
tell	told	told

INFINITIVE	PAST TENSE	PAST PARTICIPLE
think	thought	thought
become	became	become
feel	felt	felt
put	put	put
show	showed	shown
leave	left	left
bring	brought	brought
begin	began	begun
keep	kept	kept
hold	held	held
stand	stood	stood
hear	heard	heard
write	wrote	written
let	let	let
mean	meant	meant
set	set	set
meet	met	met
pay	paid	paid
sit	sat	sat
speak	spoke	spoken
win	won	won
run	ran	run
lie	lay	lain
lead	led	led
read	read	read
grow	grew	grown
lose	lost	lost
fall	fell	fallen
send	sent	sent
build	built	built
understand	understood	understood
draw	drew	drawn
break	broke	broken
spend	spent	spent

INFINITIVE	PAST TENSE	PAST PARTICIPLE
cut	cut	cut
rise	rose	risen
drive	drove	driven
buy	bought	bought
wear	wore	worn
choose	chose	chosen

6.13 *Lay* versus *Lie*

One of the most confusing sets of conjugations in English are the present and past forms of the verbs *to lie*:

- to recline

and *to lay*:

- to put down (something or someone)

Part of the confusion comes from the close similarity of the verbs, where to *lay myself down* is very close in meaning to *lay me down*. Most of the confusion, however, comes from the past tense of *to lie* being *lay*, which is the root form of *to lay*. Additionally, there seems to be some confusion about the fact that *to lay* is usually transitive, meaning that something must be laid (a direct object), and *to lie* is intransitive, meaning that nothing can be lied.

- **Infinitive:** to lay, to lie
- **Definition:** to put something or someone down; to recline
- **Simple present:** lay/lays, lie/lies
- **Simple past:** laid, lay

- **Past participle:** laid, lain
- **Present participle:** laying, lying

▸ **Bad:** She is laying on the bed.
▸ **Good:** She is lying on the bed.
▸ **Good:** She lay on the bed yesterday.
▸ **Good:** She should lie on the bed if she's ill.
▸ **Good:** She had lain on the bed all weekend.
▸ **Bad:** Lie the pillows on the bed.
▸ **Good:** Lay the pillows on the bed.
▸ **Bad:** Yesterday she lay the pillows on the bed.
▸ **Good:** Yesterday she laid the pillows on the bed.
▸ **Bad:** She had laid on the bed until her neck hurt.
▸ **Good:** She had lain on the bed until her neck hurt.

6.14 *Gotten*

In North American English, *gotten* is the past participle of *to get*, meaning *obtained or received*, while *got* is a past participle meaning *possessed*. The British tend to use *got* in both cases.

6.15 *Brung*

Brung is an informal and dialect past participle of *to bring*. While it is very common, it is best avoided in formal writing and speaking. One exception is the idiomatic phrase *dance with the one who brung you*, which means don't ignore the people who helped you get where you want to be personally or professionally.

6.16 Writing with Consistent Tenses

A common mistake of beginning or unsure writers is to change verb tenses and verb persons throughout their writing in inappropriate situations. For example:

- **Bad:** We stood on the steps and chatted. Then you kiss me and I kiss you back. We both sighed.
- **Good:** We stood on the steps and chatted. Then she kissed me and I kissed her back. We both sighed.
- **Good:** We stand on the steps and chat. Then she kisses me and I kiss her back. We both sigh.
- **Good:** We stand on the steps and chat. Then you kiss me and I kiss you back. We both sigh.

Usually this happens because the writer is attempting to recreate the messiness of spoken speech. Many times the writer will characterize this mixed-up speech as *stream of consciousness*.

However, written language is almost always far more structured and consistent than spoken language, even in written dialog, and even though people do not actually speak in a structured, consistent way.

Even the writing of those few authors who seem to be writing in the mishmash of spoken language, such as James Joyce, are still very hard to understand for most readers. Plus, Joyce had a very good editor, which most of us do not have.

Our brains process the written word and the spoken word in very different ways, and the spoken word is far easier to understand when it is a mess than the written word is.

So, to be on the safe side, if the action all happens at the same time and place with the same people, stick to consistent verb tenses and verb persons.

There are appropriate writing situations in which to change tense, such as when reporting on something that has happened, predicting something that will happen, discussing possibilities, or when dialog and narration are written together.

- As I remember it, we fought past their defensive line and dropped the ball at the four-yard line, but I'm not sure if we scored a touchdown.
- I guess we would never have forgotten the luggage if it hadn't been raining.

6.16.1 CHOOSING YOUR TENSE

Deciding what tense to write in can be difficult. You may read academic writing written in the present, past, and historical present tenses, or a mix of all three.

It is said that books, paintings, films, and other creative works exist in an eternal present, and should therefore be described in the present tense. But, of course, it's more complex than that.

For most nonfiction or academic writing, use the present tense to relay facts and the past tense to relay actions.

- The dingo is a wild dog. It was first brought to Australia more than 3,000 years ago.

In fiction, you are free to use whatever tense you prefer, but be aware that the past tense is far more customary and less likely to distract readers from your writing.

Here are some tips for college essays and other formal writing:

- When commenting on what a source says, use the present tense.
  - ‣ Adichie explores the complex class and economic issues of her era.

- When describing a source's dated, published work, use the past tense.
  - ‣ *Blue Highways* was originally published in 1982.

- When discussing current thinking of a domain or field, use the present tense.
  - ‣ Experts now believe many illnesses are made worse by stress.

- When narrating a chain of events, use the past tense.
  - ‣ The same year that France's Academy of Science refused to grant her membership for being a woman, she was awarded a Nobel Prize in chemistry.

- When narrating an exciting chain of events that lead to a big conclusion, consider using the historical present tense. This uses verbs conjugated as if they are the present tense in past tense situations.
  - ‣ After he beheads him, Shiva then puts the elephant head on Ganesha's neck.

6.17 Phrasal Verbs

Sometimes a verb becomes joined with a preposition or adverb into a new phrase that has its own meaning above and beyond its parts. This type of idiom is known as a **phrasal verb**. Phrasal verbs that are made of a verb plus a preposition are particularly difficult for English learners because it's difficult to remember which preposition is needed. Also, because these phrases are idiomatic, it may be difficult to discern any meaning in the preposition, which in turn makes it difficult to know what a verbal phrase means by trying to separate it into its component parts.

To see how different similar phrasal verbs can be, take a look at common phrasal verbs using *break* plus a preposition:

- **break down:** fail or stop functioning; collapse physically or mentally
- **break in:** interrupt a discussion; illegally enter a building with intent to steal; become well used
- **break off:** discontinue; separate a small piece from something
- **break out:** escape from prison; begin suddenly
- **break up:** end a relationship; separate something into pieces

A phrasal verb can be *separable*—where, for example, objects can be inserted in the phrase—or *inseparable*—where the parts of the phrasal verb cannot have other parts of speech inserted. Some phrasal verbs can put the object either right after the verb or right after the whole phrase.

- I looked over the contract carefully before signing.
- She looked me over before driving me to my photo shoot.

7.0

DETERMINERS

7.0 DETERMINERS

Determiners modify nouns by limiting how specific or general they are. They come at the beginning of noun phrases.

- *The* rescue operation went well.
- I gave you *that* answer yesterday.

    Determiners are not required for every noun phrase.

- Smart phones are ubiquitous.
- Birds lay eggs.
- Peaches are delicious.

    Usually, a noun phrase has just one determiner. If there is more than one, they have a natural order. Not all determiners can be used together.

- That car has *all the* right curves in *all the* right places.
- *The last* bus arrives in ten minutes.
- *My next three* magic tricks will astound you.

    Determiners include:

- **Articles.** See section 8.5, Definite and Indefinite Articles with Nouns.
- **Demonstratives.** See section 10.7, Demonstrative Pronouns and Adjectives.
- **Possessives.** See section 8.2, Possessives; section 4.6, Proper Nouns that End in *S*; and section 4.7, Common Possessive Mistakes to Avoid.

- **Quantifiers.** See section 8.4, Count Nouns and Non-Count Nouns. Quantifiers tell us how much or how many, including certain uses of numbers. They include words like

  ▶ all   ▶ many

  ▶ any   ▶ most

  ▶ every   ▶ much

  ▶ few   ▶ no

  ▶ little   ▶ some

- **Interrogative determiners.** These are *what*, *which*, and *whose*.

  ▶ *What* movie should we see tonight?

  ▶ *Which* tree is a maple?

  ▶ *Whose* jacket is this?

8.0

NOUNS

WORDS

A **common noun** is a word that indicates a person, place, thing, or idea. A **proper noun** is a specific one of those.

Among its other roles, a noun is often the *subject* of a sentence—the thing that is doing the verb—or it can be the *object*—the thing that is being acted upon by the subject.

Nouns sometimes behave like adjectives when they appear in a modifying position before another noun:

- The bicycle tire has an air leak.

Bicycle is a noun modifying the noun *tire* to tell us what kind of tire it is, and *air* is a noun modifying the noun *leak* to tell us what kind of leak it is.

8.1 Compound Nouns

Sometime nouns appearing together, or even with other parts of speech, become idiomatic **compound nouns**, so that they travel in the language together. By idiomatic I mean they behave as a unit and, to a lesser or greater degree, amount to more than the sum of their parts.

- ice cream
- coffee shop
- courthouse
- football
- payday
- well-being
- Johnny-come-lately
- mother-in-law

The first two examples above are called *open compounds*, as there is a space between the words. The third and fourth are *closed compounds*: the space between the words has been removed, but we still have an understanding of each half as an independent word that contributes its own meaning. The last two are hyphenated. As you can see, in some cases a compound includes more than two words.

Especially in North American English, the slow trend is for more compounds to be closed, and for far fewer hyphenated forms to be used, even over recent decades. Among style guides and dictionaries, you will find wide variability. For example, these are the preferred forms of several related compounds from a bunch of different dictionaries.

- firebomb
- fire drill
- fire extinguisher/fire-extinguisher
- firefighter

- fire hose
- firehouse
- fire-sale/fire sale
- fire truck
- firewall

Compounds made with two or more nouns are far more likely to be closed. In many cases, the first noun of a compound began as an *attributive noun*, which acts like an adjective in describing the second noun of the pair.

- daybed
- houseboat
- toothpaste

If the compound is made out of an adjective and a noun, it is unlikely to be hyphenated.

- middle class
- full moon
- black eye

If the last word in the compound is obviously derived from a verb, and refers to a person who does a specific type of thing, then you can often use a hyphen, especially if the word is not very common.

- fire-breather
- fire-walker
- fire-watcher

If any of the words in the compound are the *-ing* form of a verb, it is likely to be an open compound.

- driving school
- dry cleaning
- swimming pool

This is one of those rare cases where you may be able to trust your spellchecker (spell-checker?), because at least it will be consistent and not out on the forefront of closing compounds and eliminating hyphens. Also, as you read more, you'll begin to absorb which is correct for which words.

The widespread decrease of hyphenation is unfortunate, as it is very much needed in some modifying compounds. For example, the difference between these two is made clearer:

- **Good:** new hat-seller = The person who sells hats is new to the job.
- **Good:** new-hat seller = The person sells new hats.
- **Bad:** new hat seller = More context is needed to understand the exact meaning.

These are not academic distinctions, either, but widespread difficulties caused by the absence of hyphenation. Take this wording from a box of plastic bags my wife and I found in the store:

- 30 gallon bags

Because there was no hyphenation, there was a chance we could be confused. We didn't know which was meant:

- 30-gallon bags = Each bag is 30 gallons in size.
- 30 gallon-bags = There are 30 one-gallon bags.

8.2 Possessives

In English, we show ownership of a thing by changing the ending of the word for that thing, or by using *of* in a particular way.

For most singular nouns, we simply add an apostrophe (') and -*s*:

- country → country's border
- house → house's garage
- woman → woman's education

For nouns that already end in -*s*, either because that's how they're spelled or because they're plural, we can add just an apostrophe, though some style guides add -'*s* to singular nouns that end in -*s*:

- chess → chess' rule or chess's rule
- birds → birds' wings
- programs → programs' schedule
- senators → senators' election

    See section 4.6 on making names that end in -*s* possessive. You can also use -'*s* to show ownership of a whole phrase:

- *the amazing new product's* price
- *the ancient Chinese statue's* height

Sometimes in English we use *of* to show possession, but it is mainly for relationships, for extreme emphasis of ownership, or when a series of things possessing things is trying to be explained. These constructions are often awkward and, if overused, can be confusing.

- a friend of Meghan = Meghan's friend
- not a single employee of this company is permitted = no company employee is permitted
- the cat of the man of Orchard Road = the Orchard Road man's cat

As you can see in the third example, *of* can also indicate association rather than ownership: *of Orchard Road*. That association can also be expressed through the use of an attributive noun, where the noun is behaving like an adjective: *Orchard Road man*.

8.3 Collective Nouns

Collective nouns name groups of things, people, or animals.

- army
- audience
- batch
- board
- class
- committee
- company
- department

- family
- firm
- herd
- majority
- public
- school
- team

Even though a collective noun contains two or more members, in North American English it behaves as a singular. I specify "North American English" because in the United Kingdom and some other English-speaking countries, a collective noun can behave like a plural.

- **Good in US, Bad in UK:** The army is ready for maneuvers. The team is playing as never before.
- **Good in UK, Bad in US:** The army are ready for maneuvers. The team are playing as never before.

If the individual members of a collective noun are not acting together, you can use the plural verb form with the collective noun as if it were a normal plural.

- The committee are starting their own investigations.
- When beginning the research, the class have a lot of different ways to collect data.

If that sounds awkward, you can usually reword it:

- The committee members are starting their own investigations.
- When beginning the research, the class members have a lot of different ways to collect data.

8.3.1 FUN COLLECTIVE NOUNS

You may have come across long lists of collective nouns for animals, such as a *murder of crows* or a *quiver of cobras*. As fun as they are, many of the items exist only on those lists. They are not used in normal prose. They are known as *stunt words*, which means language created to amuse or impress. My advice is to enjoy the lists but resist the temptation to use things like a *shrewdness of apes* in your writing.

8.4 Count Nouns and Non-Count Nouns

Groups of nouns can be divided into two groups: count nouns and non-count nouns.

Count nouns are usually discrete items that can be counted and made plural by adding -*s*. Count nouns can take an article: *a, an, the*. They can be used in the plural form with words like *few, many*, and *these*, but they don't work with *much* or *less*. In the singular, they would be used with words like *every* and *each*.

- book
- computer
- day
- seashell
- tortilla

Non-count nouns are usually a material, substance, or process. They are often abstract. They are awkward or impossible to count as individual items, or are counted only that way in highly specialized jargon. Non-count nouns are rarely used with an article, and can be used with *much* and *less* but not with *many* or *few*.

- air
- anger
- dirt
- dying
- earth
- English
- ice
- living
- peace
- sugar
- sunshine
- water
- wood

To make non-count nouns plural, we use constructs such as *a lot of* (or synonyms, such as *an abundance of*) and *much*.

- A lot of earth was moved to make the hole.
- My wish is that there be much peace in the world.

Some nouns have two meanings that make them both count and non-count nouns.

Word	Count	Non-Count
drink	Ask the waiter for drinks.	The party will have food and drink.
light	I turned off the lights.	Light reflects off the lake.
paper	Sign the papers, please.	The printer needs more paper.
religion	Three religions worship here.	Religion is a powerful bond.
talk	He gave four conference talks.	All this talk makes me tired.

Some non-count nouns end in *-s* but are not usually treated as plurals.

- civics
- economics
- ethics
- mathematics
- measles

- mumps
- news
- physics
- tennis

See also section 8.6, Plurals.

8.5 Definite and Indefinite Articles with Nouns

Articles are used to introduce nouns in a noun phrase. They indicate whether the noun is singular or plural, whether it is a specific noun or any noun of that type, and whether we are talking about a new noun or a noun that has already been introduced in the conversation.

There are two types of articles: *definite* and *indefinite*.

The only definite article is *the*, which also happens to be one of the most common words in English. It is used to indicate a specific noun, either one discussed before, one likely to be known to all participants, or one that is important or exceptional.

- The final boss in that video game is nearly unbeatable.
- That's not the scarf that goes with those gloves.
- Give him the book he wanted.
- When you get to the ninth grade, elementary school seems far away.

There are two indefinite articles: *a* and *an*.

- A cat is a furry mammal with a long tail.
- An alligator is a reptile with many teeth.

When deciding between using *a* and *an*, the only thing to consider is the sound of the word that follows the article. If the next word begins with a consonant sound, then use *a*. If it begins with a vowel sound, then use *an*.

- an announcement
- an argument
- an iguana
- a cat
- a high-society event
- a tsk-tsk
- a yellow banana

Keep in mind that the next sound may actually be written as a consonant but sound like a vowel, and vice versa. It's the *sound* that matters, not the letter.

- an FBI investigation
- a European hotel
- an heiress
- a unicycle
- an XTC concert

Note that the *h* in some words is not aspirated (given sound) so it may take a different article.

- an hour
- a human
- an herb garden (US), a herb garden (UK)

8.5.1 *AN HISTORIC* VERSUS *A HISTORIC*

Some style guides and amateur grammarians will make a big deal out of claiming that *an* should be used with *historic* and similar words.

- an historic moment
- an historical adventure
- an historian of literature

However, the above sentences are correct only if you do *not* pronounce (or aspirate) the *h* in those words. Most North Americans do not pronounce those words that way, although some have adopted a hypercorrection and have begun to drop off the *h* sound to better fit what they mistakenly believe to be a language rule.

For most North Americans, **the only correct form is**:

- a historic moment
- a historical adventure
- a historian of literature

8.6 Plurals

In English, nouns usually are made plural by adding -*s* or -*es* to the end.

Add -*s* to most words to make a plural.

- cat → cats
- movie → movies
- rake → rakes
- taxi → taxis
- tunnel → tunnels

However, for words that end in sounds formed by endings such as *-ch*, *-s*, *-sh*, and *-x*, add *-es*.

- pitch → pitches
- Jones → Joneses
- mess → messes
- wish → wishes
- box → boxes
- tax → taxes

For most words that end in *-y*, use *-ies*.

- body → bodies
- brewery → breweries
- copy → copies
- periphery → peripheries
- query → queries

Another place where the old forms of English have stayed on even in our modern language is in the form of irregular plurals.

Probably the best-known example is a plural in which the vowel changes, and sometimes an adjoining consonant, but no new suffix is added. These are known as *mutated plurals*, a form of changed English inherited from its Germanic roots.

- foot → feet
- goose → geese
- louse → lice
- man → men
- mouse → mice
- tooth → teeth
- woman → women

Frequently, nouns ending with *-f* (or the *-f* sound) are pluralized by changing the *-f* to *-ves*.

- calf → calves
- elf → elves
- half → halves
- hoof → hoofs, hooves

- knife → knives
- leaf → leaves (exception: Toronto Maple Leafs, a hockey team)
- life → lives
- loaf → loaves
- self → selves
- shelf → shelves
- thief → thieves
- wife → wives
- wolf → wolves

Note that *roof* is not one of these words: its plural is *roofs*.

Many words borrowed from Latin, especially scientific ones, take a Latin plural:

- addendum → addenda
- alga → algae
- alumnus → alumni
- amoeba → amoebae
- antenna → antennae
- bacterium → bacteria
- cactus → cacti
- criterion → criteria
- curriculum → curricula
- datum → data (see section 8.6.8, Plural of *Data*)
- fungus → fungi
- genus → genera
- larva → larvae
- memorandum → memoranda
- stimulus → stimuli
- syllabus → syllabi
- vertebra → vertebrae

8.6.1 PLURALS OF SOME GREEK AND LATIN WORDS

Some nouns, frequently of Greek origin, that end in *-is* are made plural by changing the *-is* to *-es*.

- axis → axes
- analysis → analyses
- antithesis → antitheses
- basis → bases
- crisis → crises
- diagnosis → diagnoses
- ellipsis → ellipses
- emphasis → emphases

- hypothesis → hypotheses
- metamorphosis → metamorphoses
- neurosis → neuroses
- oasis → oases
- paralysis → paralyses
- parenthesis → parentheses
- synthesis → syntheses
- thesis → theses

Several Latin-originating nouns ending in -*ix* are pluralized with -*ices* or in the English way.

- appendix → appendices (in books), appendixes (in bodies)
- helix → helices
- index → indexes (most uses), indices (usually only in statistics or finance)
- matrix → matrices

The words of Latin and Greek origin that take the plural form of their original language are exceptions because, usually, when words are borrowed from one language to another, they use the plural constructions of the new language.

For example, English has borrowed *panini* from Italian. It's an Italian plural noun for a flattened sandwich. But in English, we treat it as a singular and add -*s* to the end to make it plural: *paninis*. We do the same thing with *zucchini* and *ravioli*.

The correct plural of *octopus* is *octopuses*, not *octopi*. It comes from Greek, not Latin, so if it weren't already thoroughly anglicized, the plural would be *octopodes*, anyway.

8.6.2 WORDS ENDING IN *O*

Following are some words ending in -*o* that are pluralized by added -*es*, instead of just -*s*, as is usually the case.

- echo → echoes
- embargo → embargoes
- hero → heroes
- potato → potatoes
- tomato → tomatoes
- torpedo → torpedoes
- veto → vetoes

8.6.3 WORDS WITH NO SINGULAR OR NO PLURAL

Plurale tantum is a Latin phrase that refers to words that mainly exist only in the plural. They don't have a normal singular form, although people sometimes mistakenly think they do.

- eyeglasses
- pants
- pliers
- trousers
- scissors (The use of *a scissor* is a hypercorrection and not a good choice, although *a pair of scissors* is fine.)

Some nouns do not have a plural form—*singulare tantum*—or else the plural looks and sounds exactly like the singular form and is obvious only through context. Often these are mass nouns, the collective name we use for more than one of the same kind of thing, as with animals.

- barracks
- deer
- fish
- gallows
- info, information
- means

- offspring
- salmon
- series

- sheep
- species
- sturgeon

Foreign learners of English in particular need to be careful not to use *infos* or *informations*, which may be permitted in their first language.

In highly specialized uses, some of these words *can* take a normal plural form. *Fish*, for example, can be *fishes* if you are discussing more than one species of fish.

- The laboratory is researching how different fishes acclimate to warmer oceans.

This word is extra problematic because there are idiomatic expressions where the word is pluralized as *fishes*: *sleeping with the fishes*, a phrase from Mafia movies that means to throw an enemy into a body of water (perhaps after giving them concrete boots), and the miracle of *the loaves and fishes* in the Bible, in which Jesus feeds many people by turning a little food into a lot.

8.6.4 WORDS THAT LOOK PLURAL BUT AREN'T

Biceps (the main muscle of the upper arm) is the same in both the singular and plural, but a misunderstanding about this has gone on for so long that an adjective *bicep* is now acceptable. The singular noun *bicep* is almost there, but my advice is to stick to a singular *biceps*. The same goes for *triceps* and *quadriceps*.

Gyro is now widely accepted as the singular word for the spiced-meat-on-pita sandwich, but some sticklers may still be holding out for *gyros*, the original singular and plural form. Pronunciation of the word is similarly confused, with YEER-oh, GUY-roh, and JIE-roh all being widely used. The first is more traditional; the last is most common.

Kudos is another Greek word whose ending is misunderstood and whose widely used singular form, *kudo*, is a break from the past, when *kudos* was the singular form.

Others that you can look up in a good dictionary: *forceps, rabies, species.*

8.6.5 APOSTROPHES DON'T MAKE WORDS PLURAL

Never use an apostrophe to make a word plural. A word gets an apostrophe only if it is possessive. Even then, the apostrophe goes *after* the plural suffix, not before it:

- the buses' headlights
- the compact discs' plastic cases

8.6.6 PLURALS OF SOME COMPOUND NOUNS

One unusual kind of plural is for some compounds that involve a noun followed by an adjective (see section 11.0) or adjectival phrase. To make them plural, the -*s* goes on the *noun part* of the compound, even though it's not the last word.

Singular	Plural	Possessive
attorney-at-law	attorneys-at-law	attorney-at-law's case
attorney general	attorneys general	attorney general's opinion
brother-in-law	brothers-in-law	brother-in-law's baby
commander-in-chief	commanders-in-chief	commander-in-chief's duties
court-martial	courts-martial/ court-martials	court-martial's transcript
father-in-law	fathers-in-law	father-in-law's apartment
hanger-on	hangers-on	hanger-on's jokes
man-of-war	men-of-war	man-of-war's guns
mother-in-law	mothers-in-law	mother-in-law's house
passer-by	passers-by	passer-by's conversation
secretary general	secretaries general	secretary general's speech
sister-in-law	sisters-in-law	sister-in-law's car

And then there are compounds that look similar to the words preceding, but because they contain no nouns, they are simply made plural by adding -s to the end.

- forget-me-not: forget-me-nots
- go-between: go-betweens
- good-bye: good-byes
- grown-up: grown-ups
- take-off: take-offs
- wanna-be: wanna-bes

See more about compound nouns in section 8.1.

8.6.7 COMMON PROBLEMS WITH PLURALS

Frequently you'll see family names written as a plural on things like holiday greeting cards, mailboxes, or signs showing a house's street number. Sometimes they are written with an apostrophe: *The Barrett's.*

The argument for apostrophes like that (usually given as a way to justify the mistake) is that it means *the Barretts' (house)*, with *house* omitted but understood.

However, this rationalization is weak. What is really happening is that it's just one more place in English where folks are getting the *-s* for plural confused with the *-s* for possession, and then over-thinking it. Leaving off the apostrophe is always a better choice, as in these examples of plain plurals with no possession:

- the Daliwals
- the Rambuteaus
- the Simmonses
- the Smith-Kungs

8.6.8 PLURAL OF *DATA*

The word *data* can be both a plural and a singular. In many academic, computing, and scientific contexts, it's usually a plural:

- The data make it clear that this process is irreversible.

Professionals in those domains often use the singular *datum.*

Non-specialists, though, tend to use *data* as a mass noun or non-count noun (see section 8.4, Count Nouns and Non-Count Nouns), similar to the way you might use *rain* or *sleep*:

- The data is ready to be put into the spreadsheet.

8.7 Proper Nouns

Most **proper nouns** are names of people, places, organizations, and commercial brands.

Other proper nouns include titles of books, songs, musical recordings, movies, and video games; names of specific animals; names of planets, stars, and other astronomical features; sea-going ships; and spacecraft. Holidays and some important dates are proper nouns, too. See section 8.8.1.2 for an explanation of why some of these are italicized.

- **Personal names:** Zhang, José, Ananya, Jane, Lincoln, Smith, Beyoncé, García, Li, Nguyen
- **Places:** Tokyo, Mexico, New York City, Greenville, Seoul, Redwood City, Kings County, Nob Hill, Montmartre, Mississippi River, Indian Ocean, Southern California
- **Media:** Minecraft (video game), *The White Album* (musical recording), *The Brief Wondrous Life of Oscar Wao* (novel), *Absolutely Fabulous* (television show), *Lagaan* (movie)
- **Organizations:** Electronic Frontier Foundation (non-governmental digital rights advocacy group), Doctors Without Borders or Médecins Sans Frontières (non-governmental aid organization), House of Representatives (US legislative body), MI6 (British spy agency), Clube de Regatas do Flamengo (Brazilian football/soccer club), Alice Birney Elementary School
- **Seacraft and spacecraft:** HMS *Bounty* (seacraft), Challenger (spacecraft), USS *Enterprise* (real sea-going aircraft carrier and fictional spacecraft)

- **Things in outer space:** the Moon (or the moon), Pluto (dwarf planet), Andromeda Galaxy
- **Holidays and dates:** July 4th or Independence Day, Passover, New Year's Day, Diwali
- **Animals:** Fluffy (pet cat), Lucy (pet dog)
- **Cultural and sporting events:** Maker Faire (a technology festival), *White Rooms and Silence* (an art show), *Race: Are We So Different?* (a museum exhibit), Ragnar (a running race), FIFA World Cup (football/soccer championship)
- **Commercial brands:** Microsoft Windows, Google, Coca-Cola, Tim Horton's, Woolworth's

Usually, we can recognize proper nouns because their first letters are capitalized, and because they are treated with a sense of importance. However, when you're writing it's sometimes hard to know whether they're proper nouns and whether to capitalize them.

For example, let's say you attend a university and take many of your classes in mathematics. Are those classes offered by the department of mathematics or the Department of Mathematics?

It depends. As always, your audience matters. How important is this particular organization to the person you're writing to? Do you both agree on its importance?

If you're writing a letter to the head of the department, it's probably best to treat it as a proper noun:

- I am really enjoying the classes offered by the Department of Mathematics, but I have a suggestion.

However, if you're writing an informal email to a friend who takes mostly literature classes, it would probably be best to write it uncapitalized:

- Professor Hernandez is the funniest guy in the department of mathematics.

8.8 Definite Article and Proper Nouns

Notice that I did not capitalize *the* in *the Department of Mathematics*. Usually, we do not capitalize *the* before proper nouns (see section 8.7, Proper Nouns). Some organizations, such as many newspapers, may prefer it in their own writing for their own audiences, but for everyone else, good writing style usually means writing it as *the* and not *The*.

For example, it's better to write *the New York Times* unless you work for *The New York Times*.

Knowing which proper nouns need the definite article *the* can be difficult, and is best learned one at a time. There is no perfect rule to help you figure it out, but in general we use the definite article if there is a very distinctive noun that we are thinking of, perhaps the only one of its kind. Sometimes we use a definite article before a proper noun because it's part of the name.

We usually use the definite article:

- **for plural names:** the Kardashians, the Dardanelles, the Philippines, the Great Lakes, the Andes Mountains

- **when the article is specifying a kind or characteristic, either with an adjective or by using *of* to show possession:** the Central Intelligence Agency, the White House, the United States of America, the Statue of Liberty, the Gulf of Siam

- **for newspapers but not magazines or most online periodicals:** the *London Times*, the *Sydney Morning Herald*. An exception: *The New Yorker*.

- **for rivers, oceans, and seas, but not individual lakes or ponds:** the Amazon River, the Black Sea, the Arctic Ocean

Proper nouns for places where the definite article is usually used:

- the Bahamas
- the Bronx
- the Gambia
- the Sudan

8.8.1 COMMON PROBLEMS WITH PROPER NOUNS

8.8.1.1 Writers who are trying to make their words sound important tend to capitalize too many nouns. When editing your writing, take a close look at each capitalized word. Is it really a proper noun? Do other people outside your organization capitalize it? Most importantly, is it capitalized in dictionaries?

8.8.1.2 Did you notice that I *italicized* the names of some of the proper nouns in this section? In most US style guides, names of newspapers, musical recordings, television shows, movies, and museum exhibits are italicized.

8.9 Nouns into Verbs

Novice writers and amateur grammarians often feel, without being able to clearly articulate why, that there's something disagreeable about a noun turning into a verb (or a verb turning into a noun), so they try to avoid using words that have been formed in this way; however, without this morphological magic, English would be an impoverished language. We *shoulder* blame. We *table* a discussion. We *google* for answers on the Internet.

It is certainly easy to overdo it.

But almost all the peevishness about turning nouns into verbs falls squarely in the *if it's new, it must be bad* camp. It's simply resistance to natural language evolution. Many verbs in English have come from nouns, and yet the same few words solicit the most complaint (such as *impact*), which suggests that the peeves are being passed from mouth to ear like a virus. That is, there's nothing inherently wrong with a verb like *incent* (more than 150 years old), it's just that people have learned from each other to complain about it.

Some common nouns that have become verbs:

- **friend:** To choose someone as a friend. At least 500 years old.
- **gift:** To give a gift, or to give something in the way one would give a gift. More than 500 years old.
- **phone:** To call someone on a telephone. More than 100 years old.

That said, if you are a new or struggling writer, leave the verbing of nouns and the nouning of verbs to others. When you try to innovate before mastering the basic forms, you are far more likely to spawn something that others find repugnant.

See section 5.6.1, Noun Phrases.

9.0

ABBREVIATIONS

WORDS

Abbreviations are a way to shorten long words and phrases so we don't have to say the long version every time. They work much in the same way pronouns (see section 10.0) do, in that we don't always want to be saying a proper noun, but instead make it easier by saying "she" or "he" for a person. In fact, abbreviating is one of the major forms of language change. It balances out the very large number of words, new ideas, and long language forms constantly being created. In other words, as we make language longer, we also try to make it shorter.

9.1 Initialisms

Initialisms are made of the first or most important letters of a phrase given together in all capitals, sometimes with periods between the letters and sometimes without.

As with acronyms (see section 9.2), initialisms often do not assign a letter (in the abbreviated form) for conjunctions, prepositions, or articles in the original longer form, nor do the abbreviation's letters have to be taken only from the first letters of words. Initialisms are pronounced by saying the individual letter's names. Note that *initialism* is the preferred term among linguists and lexicographers, but many laypeople use the term *acronym* for this variety of word, as well.

- exempli gratia: e.g.
- dead on arrival: DOA
- deoxyribonucleic acid: DNA

- Federal Bureau of Investigation: FBI
- id est: i.e.
- just kidding: j/k
- laugh(ing) out loud: LOL, lol
- oh my God: OMG, omg
- National Collegiate Athletic Association: NCAA
- trinitrotoluene: TNT
- United States of America: USA

9.2 Acronyms

Acronyms are made of the first letters of the words in a phrase; unlike initialisms, they can be written and pronounced as a word.

In North America, they are usually written as all capitals. In the United Kingdom, they are sometimes written as proper nouns (see section 8.7, Proper Nouns), with only the first letter capitalized.

- anti-social behaviour order (UK): ASBO, Asbo
- acquired immune deficiency syndrome: AIDS
- National Aeronautics and Space Administration: NASA
- North Atlantic Treaty Organization: NATO
- Rhode Island School of Design: RISD, pronounced but never written "RIZ-dee"

9.3 Shortened and Clipping

Shortened or clipped words remove letters or syllables, with the remainder sometimes undergoing modification.

- advertisement → ad
- because → 'cause
- cockroach → roach
- doctor → doc
- especially → specially
- espy → spy
- facsimile → fax
- gasoline → gas
- influenza → flu
- madam → ma'am
- memorandum → memo
- omnibus → bus
- parachute → chute
- robot → bot
- spectacles → specs
- telephone → phone

9.4 Blends and Portmanteaus

Portmanteaus or blends take parts of two words and combine them into a single word.

- costume + play → cosplay
- fan + magazine → fanzine
- motor + hotel → motel
- situation + comedy → sitcom
- Spanish + English → Spanglish
- spoon + fork → spork
- telephone + marathon → telethon

9.5 Pluralizing Acronyms and Initialisms

Acronyms and initialisms are usually made plural by adding -*s*.

- CD-ROMs
- FAQs
- MVPs

However, some style guides prefer to use -*'s*: for initialisms:

- ATMs or ATM's
- MOUs or MOU's

- RBIs or RBI's
- RFPs or RFP's
- VIPs or VIP's

Major news organizations and style guides differ on this, and both styles are widespread. As is always the case, use the method preferred by your organization, and be consistent. My preferred style is to add just -s.

If your preferred style is to use periods in your initialisms, then the best course of action to make them plural is without the apostrophe.

- I.C.B.M.s
- N.G.O.s

10.0

PRONOUNS

WORDS

Pronouns are used in place of a specific noun mentioned earlier in a sentence, so we don't have to keep saying that specific noun and can say fewer syllables. *Personal pronouns* are associated with a specific grammatical person form of a verb.

The original noun is the **antecedent**. The pronoun is the **referent**; it refers back to the original word. The antecedent and pronouns have to agree in number and gender. See Subject-Verb Agreement, section 5.2.

	SUBJECT PRONOUN	OBJECT PRONOUN	POSSESSIVE ADJECTIVE	POSSESSIVE PRONOUN	REFLEXIVE OR INTENSIVE PRONOUN
first person singular	I	me	my	mine	myself
second person singular	you	you	your	yours	yourself
third person singular, male	he	him	his	his	himself
third person singular, female	she	her	her	hers	herself

	SUBJECT PRONOUN	OBJECT PRONOUN	POSSESSIVE ADJECTIVE	POSSESSIVE PRONOUN	REFLEXIVE OR INTENSIVE PRONOUN
third person singular, neutral	it	it	its		itself
third person singular, un-gendered	they	them	their	theirs	themselves
first person plural	we	us	our	ours	ourselves
second person plural	you	you	your	yours	yourselves
third person plural	they	them	their	theirs	themselves

Most of the time when we use pronouns, we use them after we've said the original noun, either earlier in the sentence, or in a previous sentence. For example, instead of:

- Can you help Amelie? Amelie left Amelie's keys in Amelie's desk.

we can write:

- Can you help Amelie? She left her keys in her desk.

10.1 Subject Pronouns

Subject pronouns serve as the subject of the verb. Especially in the third person, subject pronouns can help us avoid having to use a person's name repeatedly.

- *I* feel happy in the sunshine.
- *You* are the best pastry chef in the city.
- Mike can't attend the party. *He* wants to visit his grandparents.
- Martita has a way with words. *She* told a ghost story that scared the kids.
- Who wants some cake? *It* looks tasty.
- *We* won the high school robotics competition.
- *You* are now sworn in as citizens of the United States.
- Have you met the neighbors? *They* have three children.

10.2 Object Pronouns

Object pronouns replace the object or indirect object (those things acted upon by the subject by way of the verb). They can also be used after prepositions.

- When will you give *me* a haircut? Do you have a date for *me*?
- I'll give *you* a present on your birthday. I have a great idea for *you*.
- Congratulate *him*! The award is for *him*.
- Tell *her* that you'll take the job. You seem perfect to *her*.
- Give *it* to your boss. Don't worry about *it*.
- Grandma always makes *us* lots of food. She doesn't see enough of *us*.
- The principal will give *you* your diplomas. I am proud of *you* all.

- I gave *them* my video game console. I was tired of listening to *them* beg for one.

A common mistake with object pronouns is to confuse them with subject pronouns, especially when you're trying to be very correct.

- **Incorrect:** Me and my sister went to Montreal. (*Me* is an object pronoun but should be the subject pronoun *I*.)
- **Correct:** My sister and I went to Montreal.
- **Incorrect:** Grandma gave my sister and I tickets to Montreal. (*I* is a subject pronoun but should be the object pronoun *me*.)
- **Correct:** Grandma gave my sister and me tickets to Montreal.

The incorrect sentence in the examples above is often thought to be correct because some speakers wrongly believe that a construction like "my sister and me" is always incorrect.

10.3 Possessive Adjectives

While not really pronouns, **possessive adjectives**, a kind of determiner (see section 7.0, Determiners), are usually lumped in with pronouns (see section 10.0, Pronouns) because they are so similar in form and function. Possessive adjectives appear before nouns, which they modify to show possession or a close relationship. Because they are not pronouns, possessive adjectives don't replace a noun.

- I'll tell you *my* story if you'll have a seat.
- *Your* brother is cute!

- He played 12 songs at *his* first concert.
- That's *her* idea, the one she patented.
- The toaster oven blew *its* fuse.
- In *our* class, we are never afraid to ask questions.
- The coach will hand out the trophies after he reads all *your* names.
- *Their* real feelings about the final score were obvious.

10.4 Possessive Pronouns

Possessive pronouns stand in for subject or object nouns (see section 5.3, Objects). To function well, it is usually clear through the situation or the context who or what is being referred to.

- That green car is *mine*.
- Are you sure that umbrella is *yours*?
- This is not my brother's bicycle. *His* is dark blue.
- My skirt is the same style as *hers*.
- We know which spaniel is *ours* because of its spots.
- These are our lacrosse sticks; *yours* are behind the goal.
- When you pick up your tickets, pick up *theirs*, too.

10.5 Reflexive and Intensive Pronouns

Reflexive pronouns and **intensive pronouns** look exactly alike, but they have different roles. Intensive pronouns are sometimes assumed to be improper forms of reflexive pronouns, when in truth they are perfectly grammatical when used correctly.

10.5.1 REFLEXIVE PRONOUNS

Reflexive pronouns redirect a clause or sentence back to the subject, which is also the direct object (see section 5.3, Objects).

That is, it is both performing the verb and being acted on by itself. A reflexive pronoun cannot be removed from a sentence without making the sentence ungrammatical, unlike an intensive pronoun (see section 10.5.2), which can be removed without affecting the sentence very much. Note that not all verbs can be reflexive.

- I gave *myself* a headache by eating ice cream too fast.
- Give *yourself* a pat on the back, because you did a good job.
- Since he is his own boss, he gave *himself* a raise.
- She allowed *herself* more time to prepare before the meeting.
- The computer restarts *itself* every night.
- We told *ourselves* it was lucky we had a spare tire.
- You're incriminating *yourselves* every time you giggle.
- Children are amazing at entertaining *themselves*.

Reflexive pronouns are often misused when a speaker or writer is trying to sound formal but not doing a very good job of it.

- **Bad:** Sarah and myself filed a police report.
- **Good:** Sarah and I filed a police report.
- **Bad:** They gave Tom and myself an official reprimand.
- **Good:** They gave Tom and me an official reprimand.

10.5.2 INTENSIVE PRONOUNS

Intensive pronouns add emphasis but do not act as the object of the verb. They can appear after the subject, or after the subject's clause.

- I *myself* am a great cook.
- You told him *yourself* that he wasn't allowed at the party.
- Adam *himself* must do the reading in order to learn.
- Even the astronomer *herself* couldn't explain the bright lights in the sky.
- I saw the missing boat *itself* pull into the harbor.
- We intend to do all the work *ourselves*.
- You *yourselves* are responsible for this mess.
- They *themselves* said they weren't bothered by the noise.

10.6 Relative Pronouns

Relative pronouns introduce relative clauses. They help make clear what is being talked about. They also tell us more about the subject or the object.

Subject	Object	Possession	Uncertainty
which	which	whose	whichever
that	that		
who	whom	whose	whoever/whomever/whosever

Which is for things. *Who* is a subject pronoun for people. *Whom* is an object pronoun for people. *Whose* is a possessive pronoun for people or things. *That* can be used for things and people, but only for defining relative clauses that specify or make a distinction about what it's referring to.

- The car *that* was stolen was the one they bought last year.
- A person *who* believes gnomes are real is someone I'd like to meet.
- Our company, *which* was founded in 1995, is being sold.
- Meet Shylah, *whose* sales are expanding in four states.

The relative pronouns that end with *-ever* introduce variability, choice, or uncertainty.

- I will accept *whichever* party invitation arrives before Saturday.
- *Whoever* you are behind that mask, I want to thank you.
- He will hire *whomever* his boss recommends.
- The car, *whosever* it was, is now rusted in the junkyard.

10.7 Demonstrative Pronouns and Adjectives

Demonstrative pronouns and **demonstrative adjectives** modify nouns to show relationships of certain things that may be near or not near.

- **this:** singular, near
- **that:** singular, not near
- **these:** plural, near
- **those:** plural, not near

Although they use the same words, demonstrative pronouns and adjectives are different in that demonstrative adjectives modify nouns and demonstrative pronouns do not modify anything but instead stand in for another noun or noun phrase.

- *That* is a long way to go. (demonstrative pronoun)
- Hand me *that* keychain. (demonstrative adjective)

Neither, *none*, and *such* are sometimes also used as demonstrative pronouns.

- *Neither* is permitted to enter the building.
- *Such* are the spoils of war.
- *None* of these socks match.

10.8 Interrogative Pronouns

The interrogative pronouns are *what, which, who, whom,* and *whose*. As you might guess by their names, these pronouns are used to ask questions, although they may also have different functions as other parts of speech.

- What was the name of your first pet?
- Which do you like better?
- Who took you to the movies?
- Whom do you prefer in the primary election?
- There's a car in the driveway. Whose is it?

10.9 *Whom* versus *Who*

Traditionally, *whom* is used as the object of a preposition or verb (see section 5.3, Objects).

- To whom are you speaking?
- He's the one whom you met when you toured the campus.
- I don't care to whom you gave it.
- She's the one with whom I went camping.

However, most speakers of English also use *who*—usually reserved for the subject—as the object pronoun in all but the most formal circumstances.

- Who are you speaking to?
- He's the one who you met when you toured the campus.
- I don't care who you gave it to.
- She's the one who I went camping with.

The change in English has not progressed so far that you should eliminate using *whom* entirely, but what you should avoid is using it incorrectly. It's not a fancier form of *who*. It has different usages, and you should understand them before deciding to use *whom*.

- **Bad:** Whom shall I say is calling?
- **Good:** *Who* shall I say *is calling*?
- **Bad:** I don't know whom you think you are.
- **Good:** I don't know *who* you think *you are*.

In both examples, *who* is correct because it is the subject pronoun.

10.10 Subject Pronouns versus Object Pronouns in Some Situations

Despite being more grammatically consistent, very few English speakers in any country use subject pronouns in phrases such as *it is I* or *this is she*. The phrases are so formal as to seem stilted or, to the ears of many English speakers, even wrong.

Instead, the colloquial formations that use the object pronoun are far more common. For example, imagine these conversations:

- **Telephone caller:** May I speak to Juanita?
- **Formal Juanita:** This is she.
- **Colloquial Juanita:** This is her.

- **You:** Knock-knock.
- **Person inside:** Who's there?
- **Formal you:** It is I.
- **Colloquial you:** It's me.

- **Lawyer:** Is this the person who attacked the victim?
- **Formal witness:** Yes, it is he.
- **Colloquial witness:** Yes, it's him.

10.11 Pronouns and Indeterminate Gender

When you know that a noun (see section 8.0, Nouns) is a female or male person or animal, then you use the appropriate subject pronoun *she* or *her*, or *he* or *him*. If you don't know whether the subject or object noun is male or female, then you can use *they* as the subject pronoun or *them* as the object pronoun, even if you know it's singular. This usage has been around for at least 600 years.

- If someone from your department wants to interview me, they should call my cell phone.
- A good scientist will always reveal their sources.
- Always ask a police officer to show their badge before letting them into your house.

In the past, it was custom to use *he* and *him* as the default pronouns when the gender of the subject was not known. You may also find that some people insist on using the phrase *he or she* or the constructions *she/he* or *s/he*. However, all these methods are now widely considered old-fashioned (or even sexist in the case of the default *he* or *him*) and a poor style choice. They should now be avoided by all writers and speakers at all levels.

If you're still uncomfortable about the singular *they*, then try to rewrite the sentence to avoid having to use either *he or she* or *they*.

- Each student should leave his or her backpack by the gym door.
- Each student should leave their backpack by the gym door.
- All students should leave their backpacks by the gym door.

An acceptable variation when you are talking about a person or people of indeterminate (or both) genders is to alternate the use of the gendered pronouns when writing at length, as long as you keep to one gender in each sentence or in each closely related idea.

- When a citizen finds herself struggling to get a small business permit from the city, she can seek help from her councilperson.

- A citizen who needs to find out how much he owes in home-business taxes can also get help from his councilperson.

Also see section 17.21, *Y'all, You Guys,* and Genderless *Guy.*

10.12 Weather *It*, Expletive *It*, and the Dummy Subject

It can be used in place of a subject as a **dummy subject** or **dummy pronoun**, which is known as an **expletive** use of *it*. *Expletive*, in this case, doesn't mean naughty words you blurt out when you're suddenly angry or hurt. It's simply a word used to make a sentence seem more grammatical without adding to the meaning.

- It seems to me that you should go to bed.
- It's not unusual to be loved by anyone.
- It's beginning to look a lot like Christmas.

More specifically, *it* can be used as the subject of a verb in a sentence about a condition or situation, especially in reference to the weather. This usage is sometimes called *weather it.*

- It is raining.
- Is it done snowing yet?
- It looks like a storm is coming on.

Also see indefinite pronouns in section 5.2, Subject-Verb Agreement.

11.0

___

ADJECTIVES

WORDS

11.0 ADJECTIVES

Adjectives describe or modify nouns (see section 8.0, Nouns). They can indicate size, shape, duration, quality, feelings, contents, and more. Adjectives usually come right before the noun, or they can be part of a phrase that describes a noun, especially after verbs like *appear*, *is*, *seem*, *look*, and *taste*. Adjectives do not change to match the noun they modify.

- He knocked over a *full* cookie jar.
- Our pizza slices were *square*.
- *Slippery* roads lead to collisions.

To make an adjective seem more forceful, we can use adverbs (see section 12.0, Adverbs), especially words like *really*, *quite*, or *very*.

- He had a *very hairy* back.
- Her house was *quite huge*.

In a few cases, adjectives can appear after nouns. These are known as *postpositive adjectives*. These tend to be idiomatic, fixed expressions, although adjectives ending in *-ible* or *-able* form a fairly consistent class of words that can operate this way.

- The president-*elect* stood at the lectern.
- We asked for the quietest room *available*.
- In times *past*, everyone knew how to grow their own food.

Adjectives can come after pronouns:

- We found something *disgusting* under the cushions.
- Send anyone *skilled* to help with the work.

11.1 Adjective Order

When more than one adjective modifies the same noun, native speakers of English have an innate understanding of which adjective comes first. If you don't have that native speaker's intuition, there are some guidelines to help you figure it out. However, to be perfect at it, you're just going to have to let your brain learn the natural order from your reading and listening.

The order usually is:

1. number
2. quality or value
3. size
4. temperature

5. shape
6. color
7. origin
8. material

▸ **Not Good:** red little wagon
▸ **Good:** little red wagon
▸ **Not Good:** a German wooden beautiful toy
▸ **Good:** a beautiful German wooden toy
▸ **Not Good:** fat twelve dreamy drummers
▸ **Good:** twelve dreamy fat drummers

11.2 Comparative and Superlative Adjectives

Comparative adjectives are used to compare two nouns (see section 8.0, Nouns), be they things, ideas, people, or animals.

▪ My bedroom is *narrower* than her closet.
▪ The grass was *greener* in their yard than it was in ours.

- My hat is *bigger* than your hat, but my head is *smaller*.
- A naked baby belly is *sweeter* than a naked adult belly.

The second item being compared can be left off if it's clear from the context.

Superlative adjectives describe a noun in an extreme way, such as being the most or least, or the best or worst. Generally, superlatives are used to compare an individual item to a group of a similar kind.

- Our child is clearly the *smartest* preschooler.
- Snakes make the *best* pets.
- New York City is the *largest* city in the United States.

To make comparatives out of most adjectives, we usually add *-er* to the adjective. To make superlatives, we usually add *-est*. In some cases, the final vowel is changed or removed to add the suffixes. For other adjectives, especially those of two syllables or more, we use *more* and *most*. In some cases, a word can take either the suffixes or the extra word.

Adjective	Comparative	Superlative
busy	busier	busiest
expensive	more expensive	most expensive
green	greener	greenest
slanted	more slanted	most slanted
fun	funner, more fun	funnest, most fun
		(see section 17.9)

11.3 Irregular Comparatives and Superlatives

Just as with so many other things in English, the language has kept some old forms from way back in history.

Adjective	Comparative	Superlative
bad	worse	worst
far	farther, further	farthest, furthest
good	better	best
little	littler, less, lesser	littlest, least
much	more	most

11.4 Proper Adjectives

Proper adjectives are derived from proper nouns, which are the names of people, places, and things (see section 8.7, Proper Nouns). By *proper* we mean "specific" rather than "formal" or "polite." They allow us to summarize a concept in just one word. Instead of writing *cooking done according to French tradition,* we can write *French cooking.* Proper adjectives tend to be capitalized and are often made with *-an, -esque,* or *-ian* suffixes.

- *American* movies
- *African* restaurant
- *Kantian* thought
- *Victorian* era

Sometimes proper nouns behave like proper adjectives and do not take a new suffix.

- *California* quail
- *Texas* barbecue
- *Wall Street* wizard

See more about proper nouns in section 8.7.

11.5 Compound Adjectives

Much like compound nouns (see section 8.1), compound adjectives combine two or more words into a single lexical item to modify a noun. They are often separated by a hyphen.

- a *broken-down* sofa
- a *six-foot-long* snake
- a *no-account* criminal

Short expressions can also be used as compound adjectives. They are set off by quotation marks.

- The *"Corvette fanatic"* portion of the driving public would love this car.
- My *"Hawaiian dream"* fantasy involves a lot of nighttime swimming.
- The cat gave me a *"where's my food?"* face as he purred on my chest.

When using *well* to make positive compound adjectives, use a hyphen when the adjective comes before the noun it modifies. When it appears after, do not use a hyphen.

- What a *well-written* speech!
- It's a *well-thought-out* plan and it will work.
- My puppy is *well behaved*.

11.6 Indefinite Adjectives

Indefinite adjectives broadly describe or modify a noun (see section 8.0, Nouns). The most common are:

- all
- any
- each
- every

- few
- many
- much
- most

- nobody
- several
- some

▸ I gave *some* candy to the baby.
▸ I want a *few* more minutes to talk.
▸ *Several* witnesses wrote down the license plate number.
▸ *Each* student will get a chance to try out the new trampoline.

12.0

ADVERBS

WORDS

Adverbs are a diverse set of words that modify verbs, adjectives (see section 11.0), and other adverbs. They tell when, where, and how an action was performed, or indicate the quality or degree. They are different from adjectives, which modify only nouns (see section 8.0, Nouns) or noun phrases (see section 5.6.1).

Many adverbs end in *-ly*, but by no means all, and some words ending in *-ly* (such as *friendly*) are not adverbs.

- I was *greatly* impressed by her presentation.
- Despite being *grossly* misinformed, he still managed to find his way.
- She is *almost always* late to class.
- I was *not* surprised by the ending of the movie.

Adverb clauses contain a subject and a verb and modify the verb of a sentence.

- He flew toward the sun *until his wax wings melted*.

Like single-word adverbs, *adverb phrases* modify a verb, adjective, or other adverb.

- He came *pulling his little sister behind him*.
- We were afraid *beyond reason*.
- We walked *very willingly* into the cold water.
- In this house, cake is gone *only too soon*.

Some words are the same whether they are used as an adverb or an adjective.

- We tried *hard*.
- Our train ran *late*.
- The speedboat zooms *fast*.

12.1 Conjunctive Adverbs

Conjunctive adverbs connect phrases (see section 5.6) or independent clauses (see section 5.4, Clauses) together. They provide transitions between ideas and show relationships.

Typically, we use a semicolon before a conjunctive adverb, unless it starts a new sentence. We use a comma after it, unless it is one syllable. If it appears inside a clause, it may be best set off by commas.

- It rained last night. *Nonetheless*, the baseball game has not been canceled.
- It remains to be seen, *however*, if the umpires will show.
- Last season we were rained out three times; *consequently*, I only got to pitch twice.

- also
- consequently
- finally
- furthermore
- hence
- however
- indeed
- likewise

- moreover
- nevertheless
- nonetheless
- otherwise
- similarly
- then
- therefore
- thus

12.2 Sentence Adverbs

A **sentence adverb** starts and modifies an entire sentence or clause (see section 5.4, Clauses).

- *Hopefully*, we will be able to see the new baby today.
- *Apparently*, all the tea in China is a lot of tea.
- *Certainly*, no one thought the dogs would be frightened by the fireworks.

A number of people writing on the subject of language insist that *hopefully* should never be used at the beginning of a sentence. Instead, they prefer that we write *it is hoped*.

However, using *hopefully* as a sentence adverb is perfectly grammatical and has been practiced by the most-educated and highest elites in the English-speaking world for centuries. You would be well within your rights to use it whenever you please.

There's just one problem: because the utterly incorrect advice has spread so far for so long, if you use *hopefully* at the beginning of a sentence, you are likely to draw attention to that instead of to your overall writing. Remember, we want people to focus on our message and not on the way we deliver it.

Therefore, avoid using *hopefully* as a sentence adverb for now. Hopefully, in a hundred years or so the myth about *hopefully* will have vanished and we will be able to use it without worrying about being criticized by well-meaning but wrong people.

For advice on avoiding adverb overuse, see section 17.1, Avoiding Adverbs.

13.0

PREPOSITIONS

WORDS

Prepositions explain relationships of space, sequence, and logic between the object of the sentence and the rest of the sentence. They help us understand connections, positions, order, and time.

Prepositions are linguistically interesting in a few key ways. First, they represent a *closed class*, meaning that new prepositions are very rarely added to the language. We use what we have. Second, prepositions have just one form. They don't take a plural (see section 8.6, Plurals), a possessive (see section 8.2, Possessives), an inflection, or anything else.

Each preposition can have many different uses, and their appearance in phrasal verbs (which is different than a verb phrase; see section 5.6, Phrases) can be easy to confuse with regular prepositional use.

In particular, *about*, *at*, *for*, and *on* are troublesome for those learning English as an additional language. For one thing, there is usually no perfect one-to-one correspondence between the prepositions in one language and the prepositions in another. Where English uses *to*, another language might use three other words, or vice versa. For another, even in English there may be regional or dialect differences.

Prepositions may be one, two, three, or even more words. We can call the multiword prepositions *phrasal prepositions* (not to be confused with prepositional phrases; see section 5.6.3).

There are three main roles for prepositional phrases.

1. They can function as *nouns* following forms of the verb *to be*.
   ▸ Her hat is *under her chair.*
   ▸ Water is *on Mars.*

2. They can function as *adverbs* modifying verbs, just as ordinary adverbs do.
   ‣ We split up *without a plan for meeting up again later.*
   ‣ This rope does not *break under heavy loads.*
3. They can function as *adjectives* modifying nouns.
   ‣ The car *next to mine* was left running.
   ‣ It rained *after my pool party.*

13.1 Common Prepositions

- about
- according to
- after
- against
- ahead of
- among
- apart from
- around
- as
- at
- because of
- before
- between
- beyond
- by
- by means of
- contrary to
- due to
- during
- for
- from
- in
- in addition to
- in front of
- in order to
- in reference to
- in regard to
- in spite of
- instead of
- into
- like
- near

- of
- on
- on account of
- on top of
- out
- out of
- over
- prior to
- pursuant to
- rather than

- such as
- through
- to
- toward
- under
- with
- with regard to
- with the exception of
- without

Also see section 17.2, *Bored Of* versus *Bored By* versus *Bored With*, and section 17.12, *On Accident* versus *By Accident*.

14.0

CONJUNCTIONS

WORDS

Conjunctions join clauses, phrases, and words together to help make sentences.

14.1 Coordinating Conjunctions

Coordinating conjunctions join two words, phrases, or independent clauses (see section 5.4, Clauses) that are parallel in structure. The seven coordinating conjunctions are by far the most common conjunctions:

- and
- but
- for
- nor

- or
- so
- yet

▸ We shouldered our packs *and* set off up the mountain.
▸ Which costume do you want, ghost *or* vampire?
▸ I washed the dishes *and* my husband dried.

Also see section 17.6, Conjunctions at the Beginning of a Sentence.

14.2 Correlative Conjunctions

Correlative conjunctions use sets of words in a parallel sentence structure to contrast or compare equal parts of a sentence. Correlative conjunctions include:

- both / and
- either / or
- neither / nor

- not / but
- not only / but also
- whether / or

▸ *Neither* the banks *nor* the post office were open because of the holiday.

▸ I want *both* butterscotch *and* chocolate sprinkles on my ice cream.

▸ She won *not only* the 100-meter race *but also* the 400-meter race.

14.3 Subordinating Conjunctions

Subordinating conjunctions are an everyday part of the language, but they may be difficult for you to break out of the surrounding clauses. They introduce dependent clauses and connect them to independent clauses (see section 5.4, Clauses). The first word of the dependent clause is the subordinating conjunction.

Here are some words and phrases that can act as subordinating conjunctions:

- after
- although
- as
- as long as
- because
- before
- even if
- if

- once
- now that
- though
- unless
- until
- when
- where
- while

As you can see in this list, subordinating conjunctions tend to help with things like the order of events, cause and effect, and conditional scenarios.

- Guthrie made breakfast *while* Sarah slept in.
- *Even though* the weather was cold, they still went hiking.
- *Once* we emptied the house, the painters began.

Some subordinating conjunctions, such as *since*, *as*, *before*, *if*, and *when*, can be modified by an adverb (see section 12.0, Adverbs).

- *Just as* we arrived at the beach, a storm moved in.
- I noticed the crack in the cup *right before* I saw the leaking coffee.

15.0

INTERJECTIONS

WORDS

Interjections are a kind of exclamation inserted into regular speech.

Interjections have a special place in English: they don't have a grammatical function, they usually cannot be inflected or modified, they do not have to be related to the other parts of the sentence, and they are highly context-sensitive. In spoken language, interjections are the words we blurt out when something unexpected has happened. They're the kinds of words we don't have to think about first.

Interjections are not usually appropriate for formal speech or writing.

It's no coincidence that interjections often appear in the company of exclamation marks (see section 16.4). Just as with that punctuation, unsophisticated writers tend to overuse interjections to show emotion. However, interjections are often blunt instruments and far less effective than using a subtler arrangement of the right nouns, verbs, adjectives, and adverbs.

Interjections have at least four roles.

1. Express mood, emotions, and feeling, especially suddenly, or especially with emphasis. There are many taboo words that fall under this usage, which we will leave for the reader to discover.

   ▸ *Wow!* That's an amazing rainbow.
   ▸ *Aw*, I wanted ice cream but someone has eaten it all.
   ▸ *What?* You never told me you were engaged to be married!
   ▸ *Damn!* Somebody made $1,000 in charges on my credit card.
   ▸ Not sure about eating ostrich meat, *huh?*

2. Interrupt a conversation or a thought, or hold someone's attention for a moment.

   ▸ Your, *um*, jeans zipper is undone.

   ▸ I'm, *uh*, trying to ask you out on a date, in case you couldn't tell.

   ▸ *Well*, I don't know what to think. She said he would be here.

3. Express yes or no.

   ▸ *Yes!* I will most definitely do it.

   ▸ *Nah*, I don't think we're going. We'd rather stay home.

   ▸ *Nope, nope, nope.* I'm not going in there until the spiders are gone.

4. Get someone's attention.

   ▸ *Yo*, Vinny! Get in the car!

   ▸ *Hey!* Will you throw that ball back over the fence?

   ▸ *Yoo-hoo!* Anyone home?

Although there are many words that can be interjections, in the right context, many other words can act as one.

- *Pizza!* You can't be serious? You don't like it?
- *Oh, habibi!* You always know how to make me happy.

15.1 Common Interjections

Here are some common interjections (in addition to the ones used in the preceding examples), with an approximate definition of their connotations.

- **ah:** a little surprise
- **aha:** a larger surprise
- **alas:** regret
- **amen:** religious affirmation

- **boo:** disappointment (or an attempt to scare someone)
- **dang:** anger or frustration
- **duh:** criticism for being dumb
- **eh:** uncertainty
- **gee:** gentle surprise

- **shucks:** self-deprecation
- **ugh:** mild disgust or dislike
- **whoops:** minor mistake
- **yay:** pleasure at an outcome
- **yikes:** mild surprise and fear

16.0

PUNCTUATION

PUNCTUATION

Thousands of years ago, there was no punctuation in any of the languages from which English is derived. But along the way, in order to make the written word better reflect the spoken word, punctuation, capitalization, and spacing were introduced to help a reader separate words and ideas from each other, and to better reflect the natural rhythms that occur in the spoken language.

16.1 Period

Also called the *full stop*, the period is the way we end sentences in English. Looking at it another way, it's also how we separate sentences so they don't run into each other. You put a period where a complete idea ends.

Also see section 17.16, Spaces after a Period.

The dot that appears in writing out some numbers, such as dollars and cents, is not called a period, but a **decimal point**, or just a **point**. They look the same but are treated differently.

For using periods in abbreviations, see section 9.0, Abbreviations.

16.2 Comma

What a useful thing a comma is! It is important to making written English easy to read, and it has many roles.

You may have learned that commas add breathing room to sentences, so that your thoughts aren't all jumbled up. That makes it sound, however, as if you just throw in a comma whenever you've been going on too long. But that's not the case. There are general guidelines about using commas that are more about organizing the parts of our sentences than they are about forcing someone to pause while reading.

16.2.1 COMMAS AND INDEPENDENT CLAUSES

In general, commas separate independent clauses (see section 5.4, Clauses) when they are connected by certain coordinating conjunctions (see section 14.1, Coordinating Conjunctions).

- We finished dinner in silence, but I knew I would have to apologize.
- She wanted to help her dry garden, so she invented her own rain dance.

16.2.2 COMMAS AND INTRODUCTORY CLAUSES

Commas are also used after introductory clauses, such as in sentences where ideas are related but set off by great contrast, where they show cause and effect, where they indicate the order of events, or where an existing condition is introduced as the background to an event.

Participial phrases in particular require a comma.

- If you take off your jacket, you'll be much cooler.
- Being of sound mind and body, I leave all my worldly goods to my wife.
- Before you start building the furniture, you had better read the instructions.
- When you draft a string along the floor, the cats will always pounce on it.

Sometimes commas are not used in sentences like these. But if you do decide not to use them in these circumstances, read the sentence aloud to yourself to make sure there's no room for confusion.

16.2.3 COMMAS AND INTERJECTIONS

Many interjections are set off by commas. See section 15.0, Interjections.

Similarly, commas are used in *tag questions*, which are usually a confirming restatement of a sentence's overall idea.

- We're ready to go, aren't we?
- They'll never fit that couch up those stairs, will they?

16.2.4 COMMAS AND VOCATIVE USES

We also use commas in *vocative* uses, which is when we call someone by name or directly refer to them.

- Hey, Joe, what's happening?
- Listen, Li, there's no telling what the market will do.
- You know, kid, you're a lot tougher than I was at your age.

16.2.5 COMMAS AND NONESSENTIAL IDEAS

We can also use commas to insert nonessential ideas or facts in the form of words, phrases, or clauses into a sentence.

Usually, these parenthetical insertions can be removed and leave the sentence grammatical.

- There's a place in Brooklyn, just across the river, where they serve the best pizza.
    - I'm going to suggest, if that's okay, that you let me help you.

16.2.6 COMMAS AND ESSENTIAL IDEAS

A common mistake is for writers to use commas to offset or enclose *essential* ideas, ones that you can't remove without ruining the sentence.

For instance, if you have a clause following a noun and beginning with *that*, then do not offset the *that* clause with commas.

- **Wrong:** I found a book, that I wanted, at the thrift store.
- **Right:** I found a book that I wanted at the thrift store.

The same goes for expressions of emotions, feelings, and thoughts.

- **Wrong:** You were wishing, that you could see Istanbul.
- **Right:** You were wishing that you could see Istanbul.

16.2.7 COMMAS AND SERIES

Commas are used to set off multiple items in a series, including longer phrases or clauses.

When one is used before a conjunction in a series, it is sometimes called an *Oxford comma*.

- There are apples, bananas, and oranges for sale.
- Our excited, wiggly, and very slippery puppy escaped from the bathtub.

- Representatives from Brazil, India, and China were present.
- By the time the week was finished, the car was wrecked, our daughter had broken her leg, and I couldn't find my credit card.

Some style guides, most notably that of the Associated Press, recommend not using a comma before the final conjunction when listing nouns in a series, except in cases where it may resolve confusion, such as with a series of phrases that already include conjunctions.

- We drank wine, sang songs and danced until dawn.

- Funds were cut from the Parks and Recreation Department, the Public Safety and Security Bureau, and the Materials and Resources Division.

    See also section 14.0, Conjunctions.

16.2.8 COMMAS AND ADJECTIVES

Use commas to separate adjectives that describe the same noun with equal status and strength (which are known as coordinate adjectives).

Do not use commas where the adjectives have different status or strength (*non-coordinate adjectives*). You can also have a mix of coordinate and non-coordinate adjectives.

- Our landlord was a funny, generous man.
- My son's beat-up red bicycle was sold at our yard sale.
- A huge, treacherous seasonal riptide threatened surfers.

See section 11.0, Adjectives, for more information.

16.2.9 COMMAS AND DESCRIPTIONS

Use commas to set off a descriptive clause or phrase that describes another part of the sentence.

- Hugging his blankie, the toddler fell asleep in the dog's bed.
- There she was, happy as a clam, telling the world about her new baby sister.
- Sitting on the pier were our friends, fishing as if they hadn't a care in the world.

16.2.10 COMMAS THAT SET OFF NAMES AND DATES

Commas are used to set off place names and dates. A common mistake is to forget to include the second comma, which completes the offset.

- Jefferson City, Missouri, is the state capital.
- Our service center is in Montreal, Canada, not far from the metro.

However, if that place name is possessive, or it becomes part of a compound, then there is no closing comma.

- Surfing thrives at San Diego, California's beaches.
- The Brooklyn, New York–loving residents said they would never move.

See section 4.8 on using commas in dates.

16.2.11 COMMAS AND DIALOG

Commas are used in dialog to separate what was said from the rest of the text, both for exact quotes and for paraphrasing.

- I told him, "Don't touch the stove!"
- "When all is said and done," she said, "we will have changed the world."
- When they asked Sascha for money, Jack reported, he said he was thinking it over.

16.2.12 COMMON MISTAKES WITH COMMAS

Commas should not separate two verbs or verb phrases in a compound predicate.

- **Wrong:** I sanded, and painted the dresser.
- **Right:** I sanded and painted the dresser.

Commas should not separate two nouns, noun phrases, or noun clauses in a compound subject or object.

- **Wrong:** My graduate advisor, and our department chair both sent letters.
- **Right:** My graduate advisor and our department chair both sent letters.

16.3 Question Mark

The **question mark** is used to end sentences that form a direct question.

- Where have all the flowers gone?
- What time is it?
- Why is the sky blue?

We don't use them when we're reporting on someone else's question, or directing one.

- She asked if we had jumper cables.
- Ask him if he knows my father.

Question marks can also appear in parenthetical items and quoted dialog.

- "Why wait?" he asked.
- We had the worst meal at that restaurant (right?), so why would you want to return?

Even very long questions need question marks.

- Do you think that even with three pairs of mittens, two layers of pants, two hats, snow goggles, long johns, four pairs of socks, furry boots, earmuffs, a scarf, and a heavy overcoat, you're still going to be cold outside?

In informal writing, question marks are often used after something the writer doubts, but only outside the sentence and not as terminal punctuation.

- We'll get to the campsite before night. (?)

With *sp*, a writer may informally use a question mark to show uncertainty about the spelling of a word.

- My girlfriend loved to listen to Einstürzende Neubauten (sp?).

Another informal use of a question mark is to combine it with an exclamation mark (see section 16.4) to show excitement and indicate a question at the same time.

- Did you know they're giving away kittens in front of the grocery store?!

A common mistake is to use a question mark for a sentence in which the writer is stating a problem that needs to be resolved but in which a question is not being asked.

- **Wrong:** My cell phone doesn't boot?
- **Right:** My cell phone doesn't boot.
- **Wrong:** The bank won't give me a loan?
- **Right:** The bank won't give me a loan.

16.4 Exclamation Mark

Also called an *exclamation point*, the exclamation mark indicates excitement, either positive or negative. It can also add emphasis, especially to commands and interjections (see section 15.0, Interjections).

- Hey! Those are my shoes!
- Wait! We have special deals for you!

Sometimes exclamation marks are used for sentences that begin with *what* or *how*, because they're not questions.

- What a good boy you are!
- How about that!

Many inexperienced or unsophisticated writers overuse exclamation marks. Often they do so because they don't know how else to indicate that something they've written is supposed to cause excitement in the reader. Sometimes they use more than one exclamation mark in a row, but even in informal writing, this is considered excessive. In formal writing, however, even in dialog, exclamation marks are rare.

Your best bet is to avoid exclamation marks. When you do use them, use them sparingly and one at a time, and consider taking them out when you edit.

16.5 Colon

Colons are hard to use well. Many writers can make it through their entire careers without ever truly needing a colon. Yet, once you know how to use them, you'll find they fit naturally into your writing. Use only one space after a colon unless you're using a typewriter.

Colons are frequently used in the salutations of form letters:

- Dear Sir:
- To whom it concerns:

Colons can introduce a series. But be careful: there's a common wrong way to do it. The right way is when what comes before the colon is an independent clause. The wrong way is when what comes before the colon is a dependent clause.

- **Wrong:** The store had: apples, bananas, and oranges.
- **Right:** The store had three kinds of fruit: apples, bananas, and oranges.

Colons are also used to connect two clauses (see section 5.4, Clauses), where the first one explains or is the logical follow-up to the second one. We don't capitalize the first letter after the colon unless the colon introduces a series of sentences and not just an independent clause.

- Perhaps the wolf will make a comeback: rangers in Yosemite National Park report a huge uptick in sightings.
- Their magic tricks were amazing: First, they made each other float. Then they recited the phone numbers of everyone in the front row. Finally, they not only sawed a lady in half, but they made her legs walk off the stage by themselves.

16.6 Semicolon

Semicolons behave a lot like periods, but they join two independent clauses (see section 5.4, Clauses) or sentences together instead of using a coordinating conjunction (see section 14.1). This indicates that the two clauses or sentences should be considered closely related. In the following sentence, in place of the semicolon we could have instead used a comma and the word *but*:

- The cats eat their meals on the counter; the dogs eat their meals on the floor.

A semicolon is also used between two independent clauses when a transition, or follow-on effect, is indicated. Common transitional expressions include *therefore, additionally, further, moreover, likewise, for instance, namely, indeed,* and *finally.* Use a comma after them.

- We love camping; however, it is too cold this time of the year.
- She'll dress you like someone to take seriously; for example, she knows exactly what shoes and watches are fashionable.

Semicolons can also be used with lists of lists, or with lists of things that contain commas.

- The delivery included sweets like butterscotch, caramel, and toffee; spices like cinnamon, ginger, and nutmeg; and baking staples like flour, baking powder, and salt.

16.7 Hyphen

Hyphens join words together to make adjectival compounds. See section 8.1, Compound Nouns.

They're also used with some affixes, such as *-like, -wise, anti-,* and *post-,* often to make adjectives.

- anti-narcotic
- cat-like
- weather-wise

Some words formed with these suffixes are now common enough that they have lost their hyphens, such as *antibiotic*, *childlike*, and *streetwise*.

Hyphens also appear in numbers written out as words, and when connecting numbers to the thing they're counting.

- ninety-eight
- seventy-one
- two-thirds
- nine-sixteenths

- twentieth-century economics
- six-stroke engine
- 50-yard dash

16.8 Dash

There are two kinds of dashes: *en dashes* and *em dashes*. Especially in formal writing, their functions are kept distinct.

16.8.1 EN DASH

An en dash (–) is the width of a lowercase letter *n*. It is used in ranges of numbers or dates. Usually there is no space on either side of an en dash.

- pages 45–90
- March 19–21
- 1904–1924

It can also be used to show an open-ended date range, where the final date is not yet known.

- Terrell Owens, 1973–

16.8.2 EM DASH

An em dash (—) is the width of an uppercase letter *M*.

It is used to set off portions of text that may be of secondary interest or even tangential. It often connects two independent clauses with a related thought in the same way parentheses or commas might, but the effect is much more striking. The em dash is usually a substantial visual interruption. Different style guides have different rulings on whether to include spaces on either side of an em dash.

- Nigel and Tamsin were married—we think they eloped to France—and then they immediately set about starting a family.

A single em dash can be used to set off a condition or conclusion for emphasis.

- We're wearing tuxedos to the birthday party—and that's not up for debate.
- The fire marshal wants to condemn the building—but he has to go to court to do it.

Em dashes can also be used to set off lists in an independent clause (see section 5.4, Clauses), sometimes with a conjunction as part of the list, and sometimes without.

- The robust rustic menu—quail, rabbit, beets, morels, persimmons, cider—was perfect after a long hunt.

Em dashes can also be used to show incomplete dialog.

- "We're getting the—," she stammered. "I think we're ready to—. Now what?"

16.9 Apostrophe

See apostrophe use in section 4.5, Contractions; section 4.8.1, Date Abbreviations; section 8.2, Possessives; and section 9.5, Pluralizing Acronyms and Initialisms.

16.10 Quotation Marks

Direct quotations are reproductions of someone's exact words. *Indirect quotations* rephrase or summarize their words.

Quotations can have a powerful effect if you choose strong, vivid passages that are better than anything you could write yourself, and that come from a respected person or expert. But it's also easy to over-quote, particularly when you have a lot of source material. Then, you'll end up with a patchwork that is hard to understand.

When you are looking for good quotations to use, don't just take anything off the Internet. A remarkable number of falsely attributed quotes are passed around, even at the highest levels, including by presidents, senators, bestselling authors, and top musicians. Even something attributed to *Bartlett's* (a famous compiler of quotations) may be wrong. Instead, make sure you're getting the quotation directly from something you know was written by the person you want to quote. I have included a very reliable book of quotations in the Further Reading section (see page 227).

Quotation marks are used around *direct quotations* of written or spoken language, or *fictional dialog* said by characters.

They are called *quote marks* or just *quotes* for short. The first of the pair is the *opening* or *open quote*. It curves to the right: " '. The second one is the *closing* or *close quote*. It curves to the left: ' ".

Most North American writers will mostly use *double* quotation marks; in the United States, commas and periods go inside quotation marks. In the United Kingdom, *single* quotes are far more likely to be used, and commas and periods go outside.

- **US:** "We are all ready for a new revolution," she said. "I aim to be in the front of that army."
- **UK:** 'We are all ready for a new revolution', she said. 'I aim to be in the front of that army'.

Some English users believe it's not logical for commas or periods to be inserted inside the quotation marks, especially if one is quoting printed matter and the commas and periods are not there in the original. However, English is not logical, and arguing about it on logical grounds is pointless. It's best to stick to the convention for most writing. This isn't a place for you to be an innovator.

In fact, the logical argument is faulty because we make all kinds of changes to what appears inside quotation marks, including deletions, additions, substitutions, and capitalization. But it all fits a standard set of universally accepted conventions that signals to the reader that something was done that may have altered the text, while still keeping the meaning and intent of the original.

The convention of putting the commas and periods inside quotation marks, by the way, is a typographical one: periods and commas look better inside or, more precisely, under quotation marks. Under is how they look, thanks to kerning, which is the automatically controlled space between characters; computers just slide the periods and commas under the close quote.

One exception we may make is when quoting software code. In that case, a comma or period inside quotation marks could be misunderstood as being part of the code and could lead to undesirable programming outcomes.

- On the next line, type "var str = document.getElementById("demo"). innerHTML;".

Question marks behave differently than periods and commas. Unless they are part of the original quotation, they go outside the closing quotation, rather than inside.

- Do you know the song "Sweet Caroline"? I sing it for karaoke.
- I think "Are You Gonna Go My Way?" by Lenny Kravitz rocks.

Usually when you're putting another set of quotation marks inside of quotation marks, you change them to single quotation marks. Again, the preceding software code example is an exception: you would keep the code unchanged.

- She said, "When we heard Neil Diamond sing 'Song Sung Blue,' we became fans for life."

When you are attributing a quote, you usually do it with a speaking verb and the quotation offset by a comma. Each speaker's turn is usually a new line of dialog.

- She told me, "There's a ghost in the attic calling your name."
- "I heard him say it," her sister said, "more than once."
- "There are too many reasons not to believe you," I answered.

When what is inside the quotation marks is a full sentence or an independent clause, capitalize the first letter, as in the preceding examples. Do not capitalize it when it's a phrase or fragment.

When quoting from a text, an attribution verb isn't always necessary, as long as it is clear from the context where it comes from.

- Gandhi had much to say about forgiving others. If "forgiveness is an attribute of the strong," then blame must be an attribute of the weak.

However, if you are naming something as a quote or a similar piece of language, such as referring to the very quote you're going to quote, a colon may be appropriate.

- My father's favorite expression: "Slicker than a bucket of boiled okra."
- The saying I like best is this old one: "Nobody dances at their own funeral."

Another use of quotes is to attribute a well-known name, such as to provide a nickname for a person, place, or thing.

- Don "The Sphinx" Mossi, who pitched for the Cleveland Indians, was also known as "Ears."

- They call the neighborhood "Loisaida," a corruption of "Lower East Side" by Spanish speakers.
- Shakespeare's *Macbeth* is called "The Scottish Play" by superstitious actors.

By the way, some fiction writers do not use quotation marks when they're trying to show what a character is thinking.

- *We're in a heap of trouble now*, Paul Bunyan told himself. *I better go stock up on supplies*.

An informal use of quotation marks shows doubt or sarcasm about a concept or thing by using them around a word or short phrase. It's not appropriate for formal writing.

- She invited me into her "castle," which was a stack of old packing crates.
- Oh, you have a "bestselling novel" on the way, do you? How nice for you.

On casual signs, you will often see quotation marks used to emphasize a word or phrase.

- Buy 'em by the "sack"!
- "Please" close the door on exiting.

Although this is incredibly common, and is easily understood unless you prefer to pretend to misunderstand it, it is also highly informal and should be avoided in most writing. Instead, capitalize, underline, bold, or italicize words to emphasize them.

When using a partial quote, use an ellipsis or a bracketed ellipsis, with a space on each side, to show where you removed text. An ellipsis is a single character made of three periods that indicates an elision or deletion.

- As Lincoln said in his Gettysburg Address, "We here highly resolve that these dead shall not have died in vain [. . .] and that government of the people, by the people, for the people, shall not perish from the earth."

16.11 Parentheses and Brackets

In formal linguistics terminology, the act of setting off text with any kind of punctuation—commas, em dashes, brackets, and so on—is called *parenthesis*. Here, though, we are referring to the punctuation known as **parentheses** (the plural form of *parenthesis*).

Parentheses add information that isn't as important as the text surrounding it, and set it off accordingly. If it were any less important, it might become a footnote. If it were any more important, it might be set off with em dashes or commas.

- Barrett, Minnesota (population 410), is the seat of Grant County.
- Naoma Barrett (née Hopkins) was born in 1910.
- The National Aeronautics and Space Administration (NASA) wants to land people on Mars.
- LOL (an acronym for Laugh Out Loud) has spawned the word "lulz," which are what you feel when you do something pointless for fun.
- My cats (Whopper and Bianca) have very different personalities.

Parentheses can also be used to enclose meta-commentary or thoughts on what was just written.

- I fear the end of the manuscript (for without its misery, I shall have nothing to fight against).
- Carpenters built me a porch, which I could have done myself (if I weren't busy).

Square brackets are used to add something not originally in a quote. As shown at the end of section 16.10 on quotations marks, we can use them around an ellipsis to show we elided the text.

We can also use square brackets to restate and clarify. If, for example, you have a quote that is not altogether clear (perhaps because the referent is in a part of the text you will not be including), you can use brackets to replace the pronoun with the referent. You can also add words that you know will help the reader understand without changing the overall effect of the original writer's words.

- **Original:** The Nobel Prize was awarded "in recognition of her services in the advancement of chemistry by the discovery of the elements radium and polonium."
- **Edited:** The Nobel Prize was awarded "in recognition of [Curie's] services in the advancement of chemistry by the discovery of the elements radium and polonium."

- **Original:** "I told him I wouldn't do the movie. No way."
- **Edited:** "I told [Spielberg] I wouldn't do the movie. No way."

- **Original:** "Goldfish often develop bacterial infections."
- **Edited:** "Goldfish [kept in unclean tanks] often develop bacterial infections."

If parentheses or brackets appear at the end of a sentence, terminating punctuation—period, question mark, or exclamation mark—goes outside them.

- We left the party early (which was just as well, as the electricity went out later).
- Can you buy me two pounds of apples (preferably the Gala variety)?

17.0

MORE USAGE
AND STYLE

USAGE AND STYLE

Besides the following sections, I have included usage and style advice throughout the rest of the book.

Usage is about the implementation of the commonly understood features of a language in a consistent way acceptable to users of that language.

Style is about the appearance of the language, such as capitalization and punctuation, as well as about its tone and register.

For example, it's one thing to know how to conjugate a verb, but it's another thing to put it into a complex sentence that not only says what you mean, but also has none of the kinds of errors that would make your readers doubt your intentions or intelligence—or cause them to suspect that you doubted their intelligence.

In a brief book, it's possible to cover only a few key usage and style points. For more, please see the books recommended in the Further Reading section (page 227).

17.1 Avoiding Adverbs

Somewhere along the way, it became a passed-along piece of advice to avoid adverbs when writing. Many inexperienced writers take this to heart and strike them from their writing wherever they realize they've used them.

However, there is nothing whatsoever intrinsically wrong with adverbs. In fact, avoiding them leads to bland, forgettable writing. You can and should use adverbs.

But, as with adjectives, it is easy to overuse them, and, like any other part of speech it is easy to use them in the wrong place. Use them in moderation and in the right ways.

You know you need to fix your adverbs when:

- You read a sentence aloud and the adverb feels awkward.
- You're using a lot of them in business or formal writing. Adverbs tend to work best in narrative and in fiction.
- You often use *very*, especially when you use *very* more than once in a row.
  - ▸ **Bad:** very small
  - ▸ **Good:** tiny
  - ▸ **Bad:** very, very small
  - ▸ **Good:** minuscule, minute
- Your adverbs are redundant.
  - ▸ **Bad:** She sang musically.
  - ▸ **Good:** She sang.
  - ▸ **Bad:** He wept tearfully.
  - ▸ **Good:** He wept.
- You use them when attributing sentences, especially with *said*.
  - ▸ **Bad:** "Those are mine," he said forcefully.
  - ▸ **Good:** "Those are mine!" he shouted.
  - ▸ **Bad:** "I am your governess," she said chirpily.
  - ▸ **Good:** "I am your governess," she chirped.

When you find a misused adverb, try finding a better verb. Redraft the sentence with a simile or metaphor. Try using a different noun.

See section 12.0 for more on adverbs.

17.2 *Bored Of* versus *Bored By* versus *Bored With*

Bored of, bored by, bored with—all three of these mean something is boring someone. However, *bored of* is newer in English and still sounds wrong to some native speakers' ears. It's better to use *bored by* or *bored with* for now in most formal writing.

17.3 *Can* versus *May*

Many a parent or teacher has corrected a child who asks, "Can I go play?" with, "You mean, *may* I go play?"

Traditionally, *can* has referred to what one was physically or mentally capable of doing. *May* was more about permission. (This is different from the *may* that is related to whether or not something is possible, as in, "It may snow tomorrow.")

At this point, however, the distinctions between *can* and *may* are almost completely lost to most English speakers. *Can* has for centuries been taking on most of the job of *may*. *May* has become stigmatized as the preferred choice of someone who is likely to correct your speech, even when it isn't their place.

May does have its uses in formal situations in which one is seeking permission, such as, "May I have this dance?" or "May I say something, your honor?"

17.4 Capital Letters

Use capital letters for proper nouns (see section 8.7) and at the beginning of a sentence. Although some writers prefer not to capitalize their first and last names, that is usually seen as pretentious and attention-seeking.

A common trait of unsophisticated writers is unnecessarily capitalizing words, especially things that seem important to them. Usually, it's best to keep a very strict definition of a proper noun, which is a name given to someone or something, and which is used as a form of address, in legal documents, or in a well-known, exceptional way. I know that's vague, but when in doubt, don't capitalize. English isn't German!

- **OK:** I spent three years in the Department of Antiquities.
- **Better:** I spent three years in the department of antiquities.
- **OK:** My major is in Political Science.
- **Better:** My major is in political science.
- **OK:** Our Security Staff lock up the building at night.
- **Better:** Our security staff lock up the building at night.

See section 8.7, Proper Nouns, for more.

17.5 Clichés

Clichés are overused phrases, expressions, sayings, or ideas. We use them because their constant overuse in what we read and hear brings them quickly to our minds. They flow effortlessly into our writing. But they are effortless because they contain little that is original, and they rarely add anything of substance.

As the clichéd advice about clichés goes, avoid them like the plague!

Clichés appear in writing and speech of all types: in every profession, at every education level, and in all genders and ages.

I have seen novice writers try to wrangle clichés into something useful, as if they could rehabilitate a long-time felon. I've never seen it done well.

I've seen other writers—some who should know better—try to justify their use of clichés by pointing out they come from Shakespeare, or they happen to be true, or they're classics. These are all rubbish arguments, frankly: just justifications for lazy writing.

How to recognize clichés:

- You've heard them your whole life, or you've known them so long that you can't remember when you first heard them.
- They have a different tone or register from the writing surrounding them.
- They feel a little empty or don't seem to add much.

A few common clichés (out of many thousands in English; google for more):

- all walks of life
- follow the money
- from the dawn of man
- in the nick of time
- in this day and age
- in today's society
- little did I know
- never a dull moment
- nipped in the bud
- throughout history
- writing on the wall

Some clichés are ideas. In fiction, common writing clichés are:

- The story opens by having a character wake from a dream.

- Characters are racial or ethnic stereotypes.
- A character comes back from the dead.
- The main character dies as the big finish to the story.

17.6 Conjunctions at the Beginning of a Sentence

They are not completely forbidden but should be used sparingly, and only in special circumstances. In short, they can be used when two independent clauses, which could otherwise be joined with a conjunction in one sentence, are, instead, left as individual sentences.

Unsophisticated writers tend to overuse conjunctions in written language because they are mimicking their common use in verbal language, and it saves having to write proper transitions between ideas.

See section 2.4, Example Paragraphs, for an example and section 14.0, Conjunctions.

17.7 Dangling Modifiers

Dangling modifiers don't make it clear what is being modified. Just be sure your modifiers are clearly associated with the thing they are modifying. Also, be sure it's clear who is acting.

- **Bad:** Outraged, a refund was demanded.
- **Good:** Outraged, the customers demanded a refund.
- **Bad:** Searching for an answer, the book would not open.
- **Good:** Searching for an answer, he could not open the book.

17.8 Double Negatives

A common myth is that *double negatives* make a positive. What usually happens is the two negatives reinforce or emphasize the negativity. For example:

- He don't need no money. = He doesn't need money.
- I don't know nothing about birthing no babies. = I really don't know anything about birthing babies.

However, that's not to say you should use double negatives. Except in rare cases, such as the one following and where they constitute an idiom or well-known thing (such as the Rolling Stones song "[I Can't Get No] Satisfaction"), double negatives make you sound uneducated.

One exception is when you are using two negatives to cancel each other out by working in tandem. They don't necessarily leave a positive behind, though: it's often more of a neutral. For example:

- She was not unlovely in her rough country way. = There was something lovely about her.
- It was not unheard of for soldiers to sleep in the barn. = It was heard of.

17.9 *Funner* and *Funnest*

Another common myth is that *funner* and *funnest* are not real words. They are! They're perfectly good English words whose reputation has been besmirched. Use them if you want, though be warned that some folks will simply refuse to believe you. For those people, use *more fun* and *most fun*. For more, see section 11.2, Comparative and Superlative Adjectives.

17.10 *Go Missing*

A lot of North Americans bristle at *go missing*, which is a Briticism that has traveled back across the Atlantic.

- He *went missing* in June and has not been found.
- My gold watch *has gone missing*.
- Won't my laptop *go missing* if I leave it unattended?

However, this usage has become so widespread for so long that any complaints about it now just come out of unexamined habit. Feel free to use it without reservation.

17.11 Misplaced Modifiers

A **misplaced modifier** isn't where it should be. It leaves room for misunderstanding. Avoid misplaced modifiers by keeping in mind what modifies what, especially when clauses and not just single words are involved.

- **Bad:** A second head grew in my dream on my shoulders.
- **Good:** In my dream a second head grew on my shoulders.
- **Bad:** The worn-out soldier's rucksack spilled its contents.
- **Good:** The soldier's worn-out rucksack spilled its contents.

In the second example, the bad sentence could be good if we actually meant that the soldier was worn out, and not the rucksack.

Only is a word you need to be careful with. Because it can modify so many other parts of speech, its location in a clause or sentence directly affects the meaning of sentences.

- We're only buying books today. = Buying books is the only thing we're doing today.
- We're buying only books today. = Books are the only thing we're buying today.
- We're buying books only today. = Today is the only day we're buying books.

Even with the correct placement of *only*, there is still a lot of room for misunderstanding. For example, many people would hear or read the first two examples above and assume they have the same meaning. They can have the same meaning, but it depends on what else is being said or done before those sentences are uttered.

Also see section 11.1, Adjective Order.

17.12 *On Accident* versus *By Accident*

By accident is the older and more traditional form. The American variant *on accident* is newer but still several decades old. Both mean *accidentally*. Use *by accident* in all formal writing and speech.

17.13 *Or* and *Nor*

In strict usage, *nor* should always be paired with *neither*.

- **Wrong:** I felt no sympathy *nor* anger at the murderer.
- **Right:** I felt *neither* sympathy *nor* anger at the murderer.

  Or, however, can be paired with *either* but does not have to be.

- **Right:** You can have *either* the chicken *or* the fish.
- **Right:** You can have the chicken *or* the fish.

  See also sections 5.2, Subject-Verb Agreement, and 14.2, Correlative Conjunctions.

17.14 Repetition

Repetition is an important rhetorical device that can be used effectively in all forms of speech and writing.

For example, you can repeat a key word or phrase for emphasis. See section 2.4, Example Paragraphs, for illustrations from published works.

Former New York Governor Mario Cuomo used repetition several different ways in his 1984 speech to the Democratic National Convention.

- "The strong"—"the strong," they tell us, "will inherit the land."
- That's not going to be easy. Mo Udall is exactly right—it won't be easy.

- We speak—we speak for young people demanding an education and a future. We speak for senior citizens.

However, one kind of repetition that may be less than ideal occurs when you are repeating a word and can't seem to find a way to avoid saying it or writing it a lot.

- He shut his mouth, but his mouth wouldn't close like other men's mouths, because his mouth was tougher than theirs.

When you're in this situation, you should avoid what is known as *elegant variation*. This is when you are so unwilling to reuse a word that you use many synonyms for the same thing.

- He shut his mouth, but his gob wouldn't close like other men's maws, because his kisser was tougher than theirs.

It's colorful, sure, but it's also distracting. Instead, break those sentences up, use pronouns, and don't be afraid of long sentences where the referent and the antecedent are far apart.

- He shut his mouth, but it wouldn't close like other men's would. His was tougher than theirs.

17.15 *Shall* versus *Will*

In North America, *shall* versus *will* isn't much of a contest because most English speakers there don't use *shall*, unless they are being ironic, comic, or pretentious.

When you do hear *shall* in North American English, it is likely part of a legal document or conversation, where *shall* is fossilized with specific uses, such as indicating legal obligation.

You may occasionally hear *shall* in formal contexts such as when being served in a nice restaurant, but one could argue that falls under pretentious uses.

In the United Kingdom, however, one is more likely to hear *shall* for the first-person singular or plural to refer to something that is going to happen in the future, and *will* for the other persons.

17.16 Spaces after a Period

The consensus among copyeditors throughout the English-speaking world is you should use just one space after a period, question mark, or exclamation mark at the end of sentence, as well as after a colon.

The main argument in favor of just one space is that modern computer typography—which accounts for the vast majority of typed writing today—automatically micro-adjusts the space after terminating punctuation so it is no longer necessary to visually signal the end of a sentence with the broad expanse of two spaces to go with a period that is not quite up to the job of doing it by itself.

Most of the arguments in favor of two spaces amount to things like "it's what we have always done" or "that's what my teacher told me in 1977." If you are still typing on a manual typewriter, then two spaces may make sense for you.

17.17 *That* versus *Which*

There is a subtle distinction between *that* and *which* that is largely followed only in formal English in the United States, and is frequently not followed informally in the United States or much at all in the United Kingdom. Knowing this distinction can help add a bit of clarity to your writing; however, you may find when this distinction is not observed, no harm is done.

Just as much confusion comes from not being certain where, or if, to place commas as it does from not being certain whether to use *that* or *which*. Even more confusion comes about because the two words are often interchangeable.

Generally, we use *that* with restrictive clauses and *which* with nonrestrictive clauses. Restrictive clauses limit and provide details about the subject.

- The house *that* is being built will belong to the mayor.
- Any car *that* you see is for sale.

A nonrestrictive clause explains something about the subject but doesn't wholly define it.

- The book, *which* I had borrowed from the library, landed in a puddle.
- The coat, *which* I found at a thrift store, kept me warm all winter.

When using *which* in a nonrestrictive clause, it is usually part of a phrase that is set off from the rest of the sentence by commas or other punctuation.

17.18 *There Is* versus *There Are*

A common mistake in English involves a compound noun of two singular nouns and the expletive use of *there* (see section 10.12, Weather It, Expletive It, and the Dummy Subject). For many speakers, their intuition tells them to use a singular subject even though the subject is plural. This mistake is even more common when *there* is part of a contraction, which has become idiomatic usage.

- **Informal:** There is a book and a bell.
- **Informal:** There's a book and a bell.
- **Best Choice:** There are a book and a bell.

17.19 *Well* versus *Good*

When asked, "How are you?" a common myth is that *well* is the better choice of these two words because it is clearly an adverb. However, in this case, *well* is actually an adjective that goes with the linking verb *is* in the question. (In other cases, *well* can be an adverb.) That means that *good*, also an adjective, would be a perfectly fine response if it weren't for those people who don't know the history of English and would criticize you for your correct usage. Use either *well* or *good* and send them to me if you get into trouble.

17.20 Wordiness

A common writing weakness is wordiness, even among professionals and educated writers.

For students, flabby writing (as it's often called) means padding the word count or page count to reach a goal.

For business people, wordiness might disguise the fact that they don't really know what they're talking about, or, as the saying goes, it might be that it's just easier to write long than it is to write short.

You can clean wordiness out of your writing with a little effort.

Avoid repeating ideas. Did you just explain the mission statement of your company in the first paragraph? Then perhaps it doesn't need to be restated.

Avoid trying to sound too formal. This is sometimes called "cop-speak," because it's how a police officer might write when making a formal report.

- **Bad:** The suspect was seen at the time entering the aforementioned premises adjacent to the location in which the suspect had dropped what appeared to be his leather wallet for holding money.
- **Better:** The suspect entered the building near where he dropped his wallet.

Avoid saying too much. If it's not relevant, leave it out. In this example, neither the make of the truck nor the make of the headphones is relevant to the story.

- **Bad:** He climbed into the Ford truck and put his Beats by Dre headphones on the seat.
- **Better:** He climbed into the truck and put his headphones on the seat.

Remove or replace business jargon or crutch phrases.
These are phrases that come easily to us yet are far longer than they need to be. Some to look for:

Avoid	Use Instead
at the present time	now
by way of	via, by
each and every	each or every
for the purpose of	for, so, to
in the event that	if
of the opinion that	think
still remains	remains
the reason is because	because
until such time as	until

Don't tell the reader what you're doing. This is sometimes called "throat clearing," where the writer prefaces the true content of the writing with statements about what they're going to say.

- **Original:** In the paragraphs below, this report will outline the strategies for defeating West Side High School.
- **Better:** Here are five strategies for defeating West Side High School.

Edit your work. Everybody must edit their work, even if someone else is also going to edit it afterward. Take a short break and come back to it fresh. Start at the top and try to treat it as if a friend wrote it. Don't read it just to bask in your genius. Edit it with the intention of cleaning, trimming, and tightening. Be firm with yourself (see section 2.8, Editing).

17.21 *Y'all*, *You Guys*, and Genderless *Guy*

English uses the same pronoun for both the second-person singular and the second-person plural: *you* (see section 10.0, Pronouns). Over the centuries, English speakers seem to have agreed this is confusing, as several new second-person plural pronouns have appeared.

Y'all, a shortening of *you all*, is widely used throughout the American South, even in formal situations. See more in section 4.5.3.

- *Y'all* want to come up on the porch and sit a while?
- I think *y'all* need to park the car in another lot.

You guys is widely used throughout the American Northeast, Midwest, and West, and is quasi-informal.

- Hey, *you guys*, welcome to the latest episode of my podcast.
- *You guys* should check out this six-wheeled space vehicle!

Both *y'all* and *you guys* are acceptable in common usage but should be avoided in formal writing.

Some people complain that the *guy* in *you guys* is masculine, and therefore shouldn't be used for groups of people that include women. However, usage over the last several decades has shown that most female speakers would have no problem with *you guys* being used by a woman to refer to a group that contains only women. In fact, if you watch make-up tutorials on YouTube, which are made almost exclusively by women for women, *you guys* is very often used to refer to the female audience.

Note that *guys* is genderless only when you're talking to people and referring to them with that pronoun. *Guys* is not genderless in other situations.

- **Wrong (about a group of women):** All these guys were crowding the make-up counter.
- **Wrong (about a group of men and women):** Some guys climbed up to the roof.
- **Right (talking to a group of women):** Hey, guys, do you like my skirt?
- **Right (talking to a group of men and women):** You know what, guys? You're invited to my party!

GLOSSARY

abbreviation: A shortened form of a word or phrase.

acronym: A type of abbreviation usually formed from the first letters of each word in a phrase. Sometimes it is made from the first letters of syllables. In strict linguistic usage, an acronym can be pronounced as a word, whereas an initialism cannot.

affix: A linguistic element added to the beginning, middle, or end of roots or words to create new words with new meanings.

agreement: The matching of parts of speech in the same clause or sentence in terms of case, gender, number, or person.

apostrophe: A punctuation mark that signals possession or indicates that letters have been left out. It is sometimes used to indicate plural numbers or acronyms.

clause: A set of words that includes a subject and predicate and conveys meaning. An *independent clause* could stand alone as a sentence; a *dependent clause* cannot.

cliché: An expression or idea that is overused to the point of being nearly meaningless.

compound: Two or more words that operate together as one part of speech and with one meaning. *Open compounds* have a space between their words. *Closed compounds* do not have spaces between their words.

conjugate: To change a base verb into its various forms needed to match voice, person, tense, and number.

consonant: A basic sound of language formed by the obstructed flow of air through the mouth, such as by the tongue or teeth. Some consonants include sounds made by the vocal cords; some do not.

contraction: A kind of abbreviation in which two or more words are shortened into one by removing letters.

coordinate adjective: An adjective that has the same strength or importance as another adjective used to describe the same noun.

copula: A verb that links other words, especially forms of *to be*, and especially one that links the subject to the complement.

dialect: A form of language that differs from formal language in consistent ways, and belongs to a cohesive group that shares a region, ethnicity, or social class.

direct object: A noun or noun phrase that is acted upon by a verb.

grammar: 1. In linguistic usage, the system of how a language works, including structure and word formation, and sometimes sound and meaning. 2. In common usage, the rules and customs related to a language (including pragmatics and style) that signal whether it conforms to what is generally understood to be good practice.

homophone: A word that has the same pronunciation as another word but a different meaning or spelling.

hypercorrection: A language mistake motivated by an attempt to sound educated or important and based on an incorrect understanding of language rules.

idiom: An expression, saying, or turn of phrase that is not necessarily understandable by breaking it down into its component parts, due to the addition of new connotations and meanings over time.

idiomatic: Natural to a native speaker.

indirect object: A noun or noun phrase affected or acted upon by the verb and the direct object.

infix: An affix that is inserted into the middle of words.

initialism: A type of abbreviated word usually formed from the first letters of each word in a phrase. In strict linguistic usage, an initialism is said as a series of letters, whereas an acronym is pronounced as a word.

morphological: Related to the forms and formation of words.

participle: A word operating as an adjective that has been formed from a verb.

phrase: A group of words that contains a cohesive meaning but cannot operate as a clause or sentence.

plural: More than one.

predicate: The part of the sentence that contains the verb being performed by the subject.

prefix: An affix added to the beginning of a word or root.

prose: Written or spoken language not conforming to any special meter.

register: The degree to which speech or text is formal and informal, or signals the speaker's membership in a social class, profession, or other cohesive group.

root: A word or smaller language component that contains meaning and can be used as a base to make other words.

singular: Just one. Not plural.

style: The form and appearance of written language, or a combination of register and usage that matches a certain context.

suffix: An affix added to the end of a word or root.

tone: The overall feeling of emotion, including positivity versus negativity, seriousness versus humorousness, politeness versus rudeness, and more.

usage: The standard way in which language is used, which may be different from what is considered most sophisticated or most formal.

vowel: A basic sound of language made by the mostly unobstructed flow of air through the vocal cords and the mouth.

FURTHER READING

Dictionaries

Above all, you should have access to at least one good dictionary. Two would be ideal, as each dictionary has its own strengths.

For American users, I recommend the *American Heritage Dictionary of the English Language*, which has very good etymologies and usage notes, and any Merriam-Webster dictionary, especially *Merriam-Webster's Collegiate Dictionary*, which is great for college students in particular. Be sure it's "Merriam-Webster," and not just "Webster," as the name "Webster" alone is no longer trademarked and can be used by anyone who makes a dictionary.

- American Heritage: ahdictionary.com
- Merriam-Webster: merriam-webster.com

For users in the rest of the world, I recommend dictionaries by Oxford University Press, Cambridge University Press, or Collins. Each of these British publishers has a very strong line of learner's dictionaries, which are written with solid sample sentences, good explanations of grammatical issues, and simple defining vocabulary.

- Oxford Dictionaries online does not include the famed *Oxford English Dictionary*, but it is still quite good: oxford -dictionaries.com
- *Cambridge English Dictionary and Thesaurus* combines three dictionaries: dictionary.cambridge.org
- Collins: collinsdictionary.com

Usage and Style

Chicago Manual of Style (16th edition). 2010. University of Chicago Press. US. Comprehensive and authoritative.

Garner, Bryan. *Garner's Modern American Usage* (3rd edition). Oxford University Press. 2009. US. Garner's work is superb, but conservative. The April 2016 edition of the book has been renamed *Garner's Modern English Usage*.

Merriam-Webster's Dictionary of English Usage. Merriam-Webster. 1994. US. Despite its age, this usage manual is held in high regard because it does away with the false rules, invented bugaboos, and elitist shaming that plague so many other usage guides. It's a very good balance and complement to Garner (previous).

New Oxford Style Manual. Oxford University Press. 2012. UK. Includes the title formerly known as *New Hart's Rules,* with the addition of the *Oxford Dictionary for Writers and Editors.* Thorough and no-nonsense.

Purdue OWL. owl.english.purdue.edu/owl/. US. This is a comprehensive and completely free website with excellent advice and help for writers at all levels.

Swan, Michael. *Swan's Practical English Usage* (3rd edition). Oxford University Press. 2005. UK. A particularly good choice for those learning English.

Other

Shapiro, Fred. *The Yale Book of Quotations.* Yale University Press. 2006. This book is on its way to supplanting all other English-language books of quotations due almost entirely to the thorough job Shapiro has done in finding the first and most popularizing uses of well-known sayings.

INDEX

W

ABOUT THE AUTHOR

Grant Barrett is an American linguist and dictionary editor specializing in slang and new words who has helped edit dozens of dictionaries. He is co-host and co-producer of the public radio show *A Way with Words* (waywordradio.org) and author of *The Official Dictionary of Unofficial English* (2006) and *The Oxford Dictionary of American Political Slang* (2003). He lives in San Diego, California, with his wife and son. Visit his personal site at grantbarrett.com.